ESSE⟩
TALES OF M
AND MURDER

ESSEX
TALES OF MYSTERY
AND MURDER

W. H. Johnson

COUNTRYSIDE BOOKS
Newbury, Berkshire

COUNTRYSIDE BOOKS
3 Catherine Road
Newbury, Berkshire

To view our complete range of books,
please visit us at
www.countrysidebooks.co.uk

ISBN 1 85306 692 3

Designed by Mon Mohan

Produced through MRM Associates Ltd., Reading
Printed by J. W. Arrowsmith Ltd., Bristol

Contents

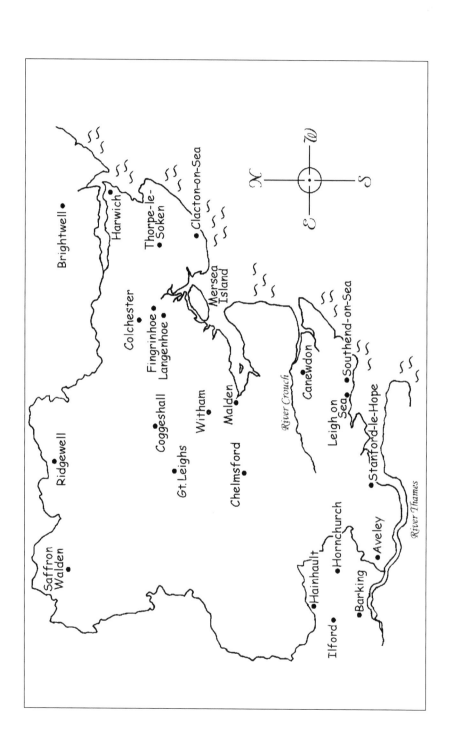

Introduction

In this selection of Essex mysteries I have sought to include as wide a range of subjects as possible. Of course, there are mysteries and mysteries. And some are undoubtedly more mysterious than others.

It would have been impossible not to include some of the intriguing unsolved murders which litter the county's story. So they find their place in these pages. But these are mysteries solely in the sense that the culprit has not been discovered.

The really mysterious mysteries, however, are those which are less easily resolved. Therefore I have included accounts of witchcraft, of ghosts, of demonic possession and of spontaneous human combustion, all of which puzzle, and each of which leaves in the mind a residue of doubt and unease. Whilst many readers will concede the uncertainties of such subjects, some will perhaps dismiss outright the account of the abduction of a family by aliens. Yet such a remarkable claim deserves inclusion for it is one of the great mysteries of Essex. If you reject it, make sure that you do so on the evidence.

I hope that readers will enjoy this selection and that it will present them with some hitherto unsuspected aspects of the Essex story.

Johnnie Johnson

Acknowledgements

One of the pleasures of writing is the generous response of so many strangers to one's requests for assistance. Without such support the business of writing would be so much less enjoyable. I should like to thank many people for responding with such patience to my sometimes complex and always desperately urgent-sounding pleas for information.

I should therefore like to thank most sincerely, and in no particular order of merit, all of the following: Geoff Garner of Chelmsford; Edwin Sparrow of Langenhoe; Fred Feather, former curator of the Essex Police History Museum and his successor, Elizabeth Farnhill; members of the Backshall family; Paul Williams whose Murder Files cuttings service has again saved me much tiresome travel and footslogging; the wonderful Essex Libraries service; Richard Shackle, local studies librarian, at Colchester Library; the librarians at Eastbourne for their customary patience; author Wesley Downes; and the Revd Trevor Dearing. I ought perhaps to absolve all of the above from any responsibility for my interpretations of the events.

I owe particular thanks to three writers whose researches have been of particular value to me in writing this book. They are the Revd William J.T. Smith, author of *The Boreham Witch*; Andrew Collins who wrote the Aveley abduction report for *Flying Saucer Review*; and the Revd John C. Dening, author of *The Restless Spirits of Langenhoe*. I am sincerely grateful to all of them.

THE REMARKABLE CASE
OF LANGENHOE CHURCH

IT cannot be denied that Ernest Merryweather was a pretty cool customer, completely unfazed by the series of odd events that for 21 years he calmly recorded in his diary. Why, he must have wondered, why Langenhoe? Why such inexplicable occurrences in this lonely little rural backwater with its scattered cottages, its bushes bending to the raw winds off the marsh, its great red sunsets and its vast empty skies? There were scarcely a couple of hundred folk in the parish, farmers and various tradesmen for the most part, and with nothing on the face of things especially remarkable about them.

Here, five miles or so from Colchester, Merryweather was rector, with an old tumbledown church whose ancient, ivy-covered walls still bore the deep scars of the earthquake of 1884. How old St Andrew's had suffered then, the gaping wounds in its fabric still visible. And when Ernest Merryweather, its last incumbent, arrived in 1937 Langenhoe church was on its last legs. No curate here, no earnest young deacon, no verger to assist the bachelor rector. He was organist and maintenance man as well as priest, and seemingly content in his work. And when odd things did happen he mentioned them to his housekeeper, Mrs Barnes, a clergyman's widow, and wrote them down in a quite matter of fact manner.

And they do seem trivial, these items that he mentioned. In 1937, for instance, the west door banged and there was no reason for it to have done so. There was no wind and no one about either. And one day in the same year he could not open his case when he was in the vestry and yet when he had left the church it opened easily enough. It was as trivial as that.

Paranormal? Well, the church was allegedly haunted, the old folk said. Apparently the figure of a woman had been seen though some talked of a figure in black and others had heard it was white. But for seven years the rector experienced no serious supernatural occurrences.

Then in 1945 there was another small mystery that Mrs Barnes mentioned to Mr Merryweather. She'd been decorating the church and had put some flowers in a vase, intending to put them on the altar. Momentarily she had placed them on one of the pews. Lo and behold, when she turned round the flowers were out of the vase and laid out on the pew. Spooky? Or had she forgotten that she had not yet put them in the vase?

It wasn't in the church, however, that Merryweather had his most curious experience. Like a good parish priest, one day in 1947 he had gone over to Langenhoe Hall to welcome the new tenants, Mr and Mrs Cutting. They received him warmly and offered to show him round the house. One of the bedrooms particularly impressed the rector. The view from the window was stunning. What a wonderful view, he told the lady of the house, what a lovely room. But Mrs Cutting would have none of it. She hated that room. She would not sleep in it. The rector was mildly surprised and continued a moment or two looking across towards the marsh. When he turned his hostess had already left the room and was in the passageway outside. And it was then that Ernest Merryweather, bachelor, walked into the warm embrace of a young woman. Not that he saw her but he knew what had happened. Just a brief encounter, nothing more than that. As he was to tell his great friend and fellow clergyman, John Dening, it was not a protracted affair. 'One embrace and the dear lady was off,' he said. To his hostess, however, Merryweather said nothing, preserving a calm as admirable as it was consistent.

There were other curiosities over the years. On more than one occasion the rector was aware of a presence in the empty church. Several times during the Communion service in 1948 there was a loud banging on the vestry door. Always at the same point in the service, always in the middle of the same prayer. Some mischief maker, some idle lads? But whenever anyone went out to find the cause there was no one to be seen.

Throughout his years at Langenhoe, Ernest Merryweather became accustomed to a variety of paranormal experiences. Some of them were undoubtedly poltergeist in origin, many of that irrational, irritating type such as when the door handle to the vestry went missing. Searching in the grass Merryweather found

Langenhoe church, c. 1952. (John Dening)

half of the metal ring. It had clearly been wrenched from its socket and sheered in half. But how? And what was the point, for the church was open? Other times the rector and others found it difficult to open the doors to the church. Of course, poltergeists often play childish and infuriating tricks with doors, locking people out, locking them in.

And what about that day when the white handprint appeared just above the lock on the outside of the vestry door? At one moment there was nothing. Minutes later there it was, as if some woman's hand had been dipped in flour and pressed against it. But there was no one about, Merryweather was sure of that.

This constant succession of inconsequential occurrences was no doubt frustrating yet Ernest Merryweather seems to have been intrigued and interested rather than unnerved. Nevertheless there were odd occasions when he felt uneasy. Mrs Barnes had told him of a time in 1948 when she felt that there was a strange and evil atmosphere in the building and one day in 1951 the rector felt ill at ease in the church for the first time. He sensed that something was trying to drive him out, that on that occasion there was what he described as murder in the air. Perhaps Merryweather was quite unconsciously able to tune into the psychic phenomena in his church. From time to time, as in the Cuttings' bedroom, it appears that the rector found himself out of his own present, coinciding with some long past events.

And what about the rector's revolving hat? One cold morning before the service, he was lighting the stove in the church. He placed his damp hat on the end of a poker in the coal bucket, hoping to dry it out. And the hat began to revolve on the end of the poker. . . Believe it? It is too daft not to believe. Typical poltergeist activity? It seems so.

Then there were the demonstrations in front of the congregation. In 1951 the altar candles became the focus of poltergeist attention. One Sunday Merryweather noticed at the end of the service one of four large candles had simply disappeared. They were all there halfway through the service and yet at the end there remained only three. And no one had seen it go. Dematerialisation?

In the middle of the service one St Swithun's Day a candle fizzled out as if a drop of water had fallen on it. Was this an example of poltergeist wit? Later in the year Merryweather and Mrs Barnes swore that a candle was blown out in mid-service.

And then there was the occasion when a bird flew around the church. The rector knew that it could not have got in for all the windows and doors were shut. But now obviously it was trying to find its way out and all of a sudden the bird disappeared. Not just hidden from sight but in mid-flight it actually disappeared. Another dematerialisation? But perhaps Merryweather was mistaken. Perhaps he was also mistaken that day in 1953 when he was doing some repair work inside the church and he laid down his trowel on a window ledge. When next he looked there it was on the edge of a pew, swinging like a pendulum.

And there were unaccountable noises, a very loud noise one day almost as if one of the walls had fallen down. Was it the tower? Had it collapsed? Merryweather had left the vestry to investigate. Yet all was in order. There was no cause for alarm. And the rector recalled how poltergeists and extraordinarily loud noises seem to go together.

The peak of the disturbances was in the years 1948 to 1952. The whole gamut of activity was gone through then. In those years for several weeks the cupboard doors in the vestry were found constantly open. Small stuff, really, but apparently a sufficient reminder that there were alien spirits lurking there, regularly active. Lamps in the nave swung unaccountably and on one occasion during morning service one of the glass funnels fell off its oil lamp base. But it did not fall immediately to the ground. It was found yards away near the organ where the rector was playing the hymn.

If most of these matters appeared to Ernest Merryweather to be curiously acceptable, he was more concerned by other paranormal happenings. On two occasions during services he had seen the apparition of a young woman at the far end of the church. The first time he had taken her for a member of the congregation arriving late but her garb – long, greyish-white dress and long flying headdress – and the fact that she disappeared through the tower wall, persuaded him otherwise. What did strike him, however, was that the woman looked so sad. Another time, alone in the church at the organ, Merryweather sensed her presence and turning, saw her watching him from the lectern. On at least two other occasions he heard a sweet female voice, singing what he took to be a Gregorian plainsong in Latin. She had been in full flow when suddenly she stopped. The rector then heard heavy male footsteps. Yet when he came out of the vestry to investigate, as expected the church was empty. And then another time in 1948 he heard a young woman's voice, heard her say, 'You are a cruel man.' A cruel man? Had something happened here?

In the summer of 1949 Ernest Merryweather made the acquaintance of a Cambridge student, John Dening, a young man destined for the Church and already fascinated by the paranormal. Hearing from a friend about the odd happenings at Langenhoe he visited the rector and there began a close friendship. Young Dening was captivated by what the old priest told him. Henceforth they corresponded and the student made regular visits to Langenhoe. Dening's links with the old church and its mysteries were to last for ten years.

Compelling as they were the poltergeist activities were to become less important to the two men than the apparition of the young woman. It was apparent to them that some dramatic, perhaps tragic, event had taken place, possibly inside the church. Didn't the woman appear there? Hadn't she mentioned a cruel man? Hadn't there been the sound of a man's footsteps?

Merryweather and Dening were increasingly certain that the young woman, to judge from her clothing, was long dead but for some or other reason, she was still earth-bound. Perhaps she did not even know that she was dead. The clergymen were anxious to establish direct contact with her in order to release her. She might still be suffering from long past events. Out of a wish to fulfil their Christian duty, they were desperate to help this lost soul.

From now on it was the younger man, John Dening, who took the initiative. He knew that there were mixed viewpoints within the Church regarding contacts with the dead, but his membership of the newly formed Churches' Fellowship for Psychical Study to which some highly placed churchmen belonged, encouraged him to consider employing a medium. Merryweather and Dening earnestly discussed the propriety of holding a seance in Langenhoe church. They concluded that as theirs was a serious task, no less than the saving of a soul, they were perfectly justified in finding a medium to conduct a seance.

It was in August 1957 that Dening invited Mrs May Lampard, clairvoyant and trance-medium, to come to Langenhoe. But he gave her no indication in advance of either the location or the circumstances. When May Lampard first entered Langenhoe church the following July she still had no information about what concerned Merryweather and Dening. What she did later confide was that as soon as she went into the church she was afraid. Only her Christian faith sustained her at that moment.

There were six other people present at the sitting although the ageing Reverend Ernest Merryweather excused himself, explaining that a night in his cold church might prove too much for him. But what a night it proved to be.

The seance began with hymns and prayers and then the sitters arranged themselves in a circle, Mrs Lampard seating herself in a stout Jacobean chair. The medium's clairvoyant powers were demonstrated first. There had been Romans here: she saw them. There was a crusader knight and an old clergyman: they were present she told the others. Then she discerned a young woman: she thought she was somehow connected with a farm and that she had at some time played music in the church. Now more impressions crowded in and Mrs Lampard told how she felt strongly that there had been a struggle here, in the church, between a man and a woman. He had stabbed her, killed her, here.

Mrs Lampard went into a trance and the sitters first heard a female voice. And then, there was a transformation. In his arresting book *The Restless Spirits of Langenhoe*, John Dening tells how he perceived an apparent physical change come over Mrs

Lampard as she sat in the Jacobean chair. For some moments it seemed that in her place was a powerfully built man. All of those present heard him speak, his voice coarse and commanding. He urged them to leave. And when the sitters told him that they had come to help him, that he was long dead and that the year was 1958, he scorned them, ordering them out. The chair in which Mrs Lampard sat began to rock violently and then just as suddenly it stopped. The man had gone.

Then came the woman. She was Mary Felicity, she said. And she wept for the man. He was her master, Sir Robert, she told them. But she feared for him, for he was a lost soul bound for the fires of hell. She called to Sir Robert to go to the light of salvation which was there for him at that very moment. It would be his escape, his release. Mary Felicity finally spoke a prayer in Latin and on finishing, asked to be blessed. Finally she made her farewell and those present were certain that after several centuries she was released from her ties to Langenhoe.

Mrs Lampard's contact came through next. This was a Red Indian, Red Hawk. He explained that Mary Felicity had been murdered near the font in the west end of the church. She had resisted Sir Robert's advances and the man, enraged, had stabbed her. She had been buried secretly in the churchyard possibly with the connivance of the priest and others of Sir Robert's followers.

Imagination? Some kind of telepathic link between Dening and the medium? Hocus pocus? Dening and Merryweather had both experienced paranormal events in Langenhoe. Both had studied the spirit world. Ghosts, apparitions, poltergeists were not, they knew, figments of the storyteller's imagination. The Church knows about these matters, knows about the supernatural, the seemingly inexplicable. These two clergymen were not dabbling in occult fantasies. They were too well aware of the existence of the spirit world, too shrewd to be taken in by some fraudulent medium. They believed that Mary Felicity had been murdered in the church and they were satisfied that she had been released from her sad after-life at Langenhoe.

Without Dening and Merryweather, Mrs Lampard's group of seven held a seance at her home in August 1958. They had no time to contact either of the clergymen. Time, according to Red Hawk, was of the essence. Sir Robert wished to speak. But first there was Mary Felicity, begging that they would help release the knight from his earthbound state. And then Sir Robert came through as

Mary Felicity, murdered in Langenhoe church c. 1600. This impression was drawn by Peggy Harris who was present at the seances in the 1950s.

arrogant and defiant as before. No, he was not dead. Yes, he was a loyal subject of King James. Dead? King James was dead? He was astounded. His name? Sir Robert att Ford. But no, he insisted in his stubborn manner, he was not dead. And it was only after an hour that he had begun to have doubts. Was he dead? Had he really been dead for 350 years? And then, finally, he begged forgiveness for all of his evil deeds. And now he asked to be released.

The story as told by Dening is of the redemption of two souls. But it is also the story of a loving spirit who stayed on to try to save a wicked man.

Langenhoe church, haunt of disembodied spirits, some mischievous, some frankly evil, was pulled down in 1962. Its priest, the Reverend Ernest Merryweather, that patient chronicler, perhaps our only priest to be embraced by a ghost – was it Mary Felicity? – passed on in 1965. John Dening, now retired, completed his published account of these remarkable matters in the year 2000.

WHO SHOT FRANK WARREN?

A T about 8 o'clock on 30th November 1989 outside the Broadway Theatre, Barking, a man shot Frank Warren, one of Britain's most important boxing promoters, as he got out of his car. His business partner, John Botros, saw Warren stagger, clutching his side, and fearing that the gunman would shoot again he attempted to grapple with the assailant. But the man with the gun was too strong and he pushed Botros off and ran away into the night.

A year later at the Old Bailey, Frank Warren was to tell the court what he recalled of that evening. He had been on his way to attend one of his own boxing promotions at the Broadway Theatre. As he got out of his Bentley he was startled by what he thought was a car back-firing. He had turned round only to see a man six feet away wearing a hooded anorak and with a mask over the lower part of his face. And he was holding a gun.

'I tried to get out of the way,' Warren told the court. 'He was too far away to grab hold of. If I had tried to get closer I would have become a bigger target so I tried to get behind the car. As I did so I heard another bang. I felt a pain in the left-hand side of my chest. I ran along the pavement and was aware I had been shot. There was a grassy slope. I started zigzagging down it in case there was another shot so it would miss me. I lost my breath and sank down on one knee. I was conscious all the time. While I was on the ground it was very painful and I started to lose my breath, which I thought was my lungs filling up with blood, and I began to gurgle.'

A doctor arrived and gave the wounded man first-aid. Then came a police van and he was taken to hospital. On 11th December, Frank Warren was discharged from hospital, aware that he had escaped death by only a few centimetres.

But the gunman, who was it? Even today, he has not been identified. Nevertheless, in what was at the time described as the best show in town, with queues for entry to the Old Bailey each of the eleven days of the trial, a man was tried and acquitted of attempted murder.

And the man with the motive, according to the prosecution, was Terry Marsh, one of Frank Warren's own stable of top-flight boxers, the likes of Frank Bruno, Nigel Benn and Chris Eubank.

On 17th January 1990, Marsh was arrested at Gatwick airport on his return from a visit to America. He was charged with attempted murder and with the unlawful possession of ammunition in his parents' house where he was living at the time of the incident.

It was inconceivable. Terry Marsh was a working-class hero. Anyone who followed boxing knew about Marsh, a true champion and a boxer of rare courage. Not that he was always vastly superior in skill to his opponents. Many of those he encountered in his 27 professional fights were better than he was in terms of sheer ring-craft. But what made Terry Marsh rise above the others was his will-power, his determination, his willingness to enter the pain-zone and to stay there until he had enough strength to battle through it and out the other side. You could have compared the ex-Marine to some great comic-strip hero, a full-time firefighter by day and on the boxing bills at night. Amateur and professional, he'd won at all levels, British, European and World, at his weight. So really, that's why it seems so difficult to think of him, only three years after winning the world title, standing in the dock at the Old Bailey, accused of the attempted murder of his former manager, Frank Warren. How could they have fallen out so badly that Marsh could be even suspected of shooting his former mentor, the man who had guided his career to the very top?

Perhaps it went back to that wonderful night in March 1987 in a great big circus tent in Basildon, Terry's home town, when he defeated the American Joe Manley for the light-welterweight championship of the world. Was it in those minutes of mayhem, just after he was declared winner, amid all the cheers and chanting, the back-slapping, the attempted speeches, the jumping up and down, that things began to go wrong? In the very moments of supreme triumph, with Marsh posing for the photographers, his arms aloft; with Frank and his boxer exchanging triumphant

Terry Marsh, accused of attempted murder, holds up the world light welterweight belt he won in 1987. (The Times)

smiles; with Frank having a word with the journalists; was that when the relationship between the two men began to go sour? Because Terry was refusing, quite unaccountably, to put on the championship belt, that great ornate acknowledgement of his supremacy. No matter how much manager and officials tried to persuade him otherwise, Terry would not wear the belt.

The next day, however, Marsh approached a tabloid newspaper. They could take pictures of him and his wife and children, he said.

And he would wear the belt. The sum quoted was £10,000.

Was this a confirmatory sign that the successful Warren-Marsh partnership which had lasted for nearly ten years was crumbling? Not that they were ever the greatest of pals. Their relationship was described in court as 'okay'. The two men got on reasonably well but what tied them together was the business of boxing. Their links were based on cash and presumably mutual trust.

After the triumph of the world title fight Marsh successfully defended his championship against the Japanese fighter, Akio Kameda. Then in September 1987 a contract was signed for him to mount his second defence of the title against another American fighter.

But the following day the *Sun* ran a story about Marsh. They had rung him asking questions about his marriage. Was it true, the *Sun* had asked in true tabloid style, that his marriage was in difficulties? Not at all, Marsh had answered, but he did have another interesting tale for them. It would be worth £25,000, Marsh is alleged to have said. He had just signed a contract for a fight but he had epilepsy. Epilepsy? Now there was a story for the newspaper, a leading boxer signing a contract when he was unfit to fight. And when the story was printed there was an implied question: where was Frank Warren in all this? Was he not aware that his fighter had a serious medical condition?

Not unnaturally, Warren was furious. Even though Marsh had passed a rigorous physical examination only days earlier this was potentially professionally damaging to him. What if the British Boxing Board of Control were to revoke his licence? What if the American management who had signed the contract for the fight came on to him? Warren denied knowing anything about his boxer's epilepsy, sued the *Sun* and won £40,000 and an apology in an out-of-court settlement.

From now on, although Terry Marsh was still under contract to Warren, whatever had survived of their relationship was irrevocably shattered. Marsh, of course, was now finished as a boxer.

After his fighter had won the world championship, Warren had negotiated with Thames Television for Marsh to appear as commentator on the boxing programme *Seconds Out*. He was an ideal choice, popular, articulate and knowledgeable. He was to receive £500 for each appearance. But after only three appearances Warren arranged for the television contract to be terminated and withheld about £1,500 pounds due to Marsh for his appearances. And there were other financial disputes between the manager and his former protegé.

On 25th January 1989, Marsh appeared on the television programme, *Midweek Sport Special*, and was again asked about the epilepsy which had cut short his career. How had he come to sign a contract in September 1987 when he knew of his condition? Did others know about it? Everyone who needed to know, Terry told the interviewer, had been told about his epilepsy.

In court, during Marsh's trial, the prosecution was to claim that it was not just these words which were important, but the way in which they had been said. There was, said the prosecution, the clearest implication that Warren had known all along that he was signing a contract with a boxer who was unfit. Precisely the same conclusions would be drawn again about Warren as when the *Sun* had run the story. But this time it was Terry Marsh himself who appeared to be making a highly damaging slur on the boxing promoter's integrity.

Angrily refuting the allegation, Warren issued a writ for libel against his former fighter. Marsh was now in financial difficulties, with business debts of over £100,000 and being pursued for £22,000 by Customs and Excise.

It was the prospect of ruinous damages and costs that was the motive for the attempted murder, according to the prosecution during the eleven-day trial. And there would be the additional personal humiliation of the libel case for if he lost, Terry Marsh, went the prosecution case, was afraid that he would be remembered not as a great boxer, but as a liar and a cheat. Against that, it was argued by Marsh that he wanted the libel case against him to go ahead before Warren was bankrupted for he too was in some financial difficulty.

If the trial of Terry Marsh in October 1990 is remembered for anything it is likely to be for the masterful defence by Richard Ferguson QC. The man who had so narrowly escaped death was at times made to appear the villain of the piece. And the tabloid press, loving it all, raked up what it could and published what it dared. What was Warren's financial position? Was he not more than £4 million in debt? At the time of the shooting wasn't his business empire ready to collapse? Weren't there writs against him?

And there was a lady-friend as well, wasn't there? Warren's

Frank Warren, the famous boxing promoter. (The Times)

private life was now public. Ferguson jabbed away. And how the tabloids loved it. Frank Warren? He was a millionaire and yet he was in debt. He had everything, a wife who was a former *Vogue* model, four small children, a luxurious home. And there were other stories about gangland killings, drug dealers. How dare he behave like that, taking on a British hero? At least two of the tabloids paid dearly for the gangland slayings stories.

If anyone in that court room reeled on the ropes it was Frank Warren, at the mercy of an advocate on top form. So, Ferguson was saying, weren't there others who might want to have a go at him? Hadn't other people cause to want him dead? Terry Marsh wasn't the only man with a motive.

'I came here because someone tried to shoot me,' Warren burst out angrily at one point. 'Now I am getting character assassination. You are going into these things. I don't see the relevance.'

Richard Ferguson said he was merely examining the possibility that others had motives as strong as any that Terry Marsh might have had.

And Warren's life-style, the kind of business he was in, did that not mean that he met men of violence or potential violence? This was Ferguson boring in remorselessly, every question a body-sapping blow, and Warren covering up, trying to defend himself against the onslaught, replying it seems somewhat tamely, 'Boxing is a controlled-violence sport. There are people in it who have come from working-class backgrounds and have been in trouble. You come across them but, to the best of my knowledge, I have not had business dealings with shady characters.'

But had Warren never received threats against his life? No, but he did admit that a boxing promotion at Windsor in 1987 had been disrupted by a bomb-scare and agreed that it could have been intended to harm him financially. He also recalled a tear gas incident at a promotion in Birmingham in 1988. Well, Ferguson left the jury to draw its conclusions. This was a man with enemies.

And if ever a man was well-served by witnesses intended to provide evidence against him, it was Terry Marsh.

A group of youths, standing near the theatre on the evening of the murder attempt, were curious about a man wearing a hood and with a scarf over his mouth. His appearance made him sufficiently bizarre for one of the boys, 16 year old Bradley Parsons, to go over and ask him the time. Parsons could not hear what the man said because of the scarf and when he repeated his request the man showed him the watch on his right wrist. Parsons noticed that the stranger was wearing black leather gloves.

When the man continued standing in the same place Parsons went over to challenge him again, asking what he was waiting for. For his mates, came the answer. They were going to a club. His name, he told Parsons, was Paul. But Parsons had not seen the man's face.

Another witness from this group of boys was John Richardson, a 14 year old. He told the court that the man had reminded him of Terry Marsh. He had recognised him because he had seen him on television and also because he once met him and talked to him in Dagenham baths when the boxer was training to be a stunt man. Under examination, Richardson said that he could not recognise the voice because of the scarf but he said that the man was certainly about the same height and weight as Marsh. He admitted too that when he spoke to the police after the shooting he had not mentioned the man's resemblance to the boxer.

Mr Justice Fennell was later to warn the jury about the reliability of young Richardson's evidence, as he was also to warn them about that given by 69 year old William Hawes. Where a witness has only had a limited opportunity to see another person, the judge said, there is clearly scope for error.

Hawes had been waiting outside the theatre before going in to the boxing. Suddenly, a man ran up and stopped briefly beside him for about four seconds. The man had raised both arms in the air in an excited manner before taking off again just as another man arrived, obviously pursuing him. Mr Hawes agreed however it was not until almost two months later, the day after Marsh's arrest, that he made a statement to the police about the resemblance between Marsh and the man the prosecution claimed was the gunman. 'I couldn't say it was him,' Hawes explained under cross-examination. 'I was just saying he looked like Terry Marsh.'

Asked the question by Richard Ferguson, this witness denied telling a friend that he hoped to obtain money for giving evidence against Marsh and rounded on the man he had thought a friend in the public gallery. 'Call yourself a friend?' he snarled.

The most brilliant disaster among the prosecution witnesses, however, was 'Peter Harris', who appeared in court wearing dark glasses and a hooded red anorak. He said Marsh had confessed his crime to him in the remand wing exercise yard at Wormwood

Scrubs. Marsh had said that he had been convinced that he had left Warren for dead. And the boxer had also told him that the gun was to be used again, this time by unspecified persons on an armed robbery, and this was intended to deceive police about who had shot Warren.

'Harris' said that Marsh had told him, 'Frank Warren ties people up in legal documents and then stuffs them right through to the end and leaves them penniless.'

It is unlikely that the jury placed much credence in his account, however, when it was revealed in cross-examination that when last arrested he was carrying twenty credit cards, three cheque books, seven driving licences, seventeen bank cash cards, three vehicle registration papers, two bank certificates and two passports. And had he not received a more lenient sentence after passing on his untrue story to the police, Ferguson asked 'Harris', describing him as 'an inveterate liar'?

Richard Ferguson did not put his client on the stand. Why should he? The prosecution, as Ferguson said, 'had not laid a glove on him'. They had neither forensic evidence nor credible witnesses.

After eleven days a jury of seven men and four women found Terry Marsh not guilty of attempted murder. Frank Warren was left feeling that he was the accused. 'I discovered that there is a terrible stigma to getting shot. Instead of being treated like the innocent victim of a shooting, I found myself being asked why it happened.'

As for Terry Marsh, he made his way out of a back entrance to escape the crowds of well-wishers who had cheered the verdict. With his head covered by his jacket, he was escorted to a van by a posse of newspaper men and minders. No-one was allowed to speak to him or photograph him until a deal had been agreed by Marsh and his business colleagues. In the Phoenix Apollo Restaurant at Stratford Green the tabloid hacks queued to make their offers. The *Sun* eventually paid £140,000 for the story. And there was a series of other sorry tales in other tabloids which raised cash for several of those involved.

And there it all more or less ends. Frank Warren is still one of Britain's most powerful leisure entertainment moguls. He has presented not just boxers but singers, Pavarotti among them. Inevitably, he has had the odd bad result. One poor deal led to his having to pay the American promoter, Don King, £7.5 million.

And although in 2000 he successfully arranged a fight in Britain for Mike Tyson, he has said that he will have no future dealings with him. There were suggestions that Warren had experienced Tyson's notoriously uncertain temperament. But in the main Frank Warren's career is marked by great successes.

Terry Marsh, that mercurial bundle of contradictions, the one-time junior chess champion, the ex-Marine who had had experience in the Falklands and Northern Ireland, did not prosper as a manager or promoter in that area which he so brilliantly illuminated as a boxer. Instead he went on to pick up a couple of University degrees and to stand for a brief while as a prospective Lib-Dem Parliamentary candidate.

All very interesting but it does not answer the question. Who shot Frank Warren?

DEALING WITH DEMONS

ABSURD. Ridiculous. We are not in the Middle Ages now. So you can forget about demonic possession.

Or can you?

Can the notion of body, mind and soul being occupied – yes, *literally* occupied, controlled and ordered by an evil spirit – be accepted in the 21st century?

Or is it so much mumbo-jumbo?

Well, one Essex headteacher did not think so when, only a few years ago, a dozen of his pupils came to him in terror. They had made an ouija board with the notion of contacting the spirits of the dead. Quite a wheeze they had thought at the time. But then their troubles began and these young people were troubled by increasingly frightening forces. Just as in another school, after a similar experiment, a girl woke in the night to find a vague figure standing in her bedroom. And a boy suddenly stood up in class, screaming at a spirit which he claimed was perching on his shoulder. Terrified he ran out of school. Yet another boy stated that he had used an ouija board in the toilets of a local recreation ground. At the end of the session some indefinable force had prevented him from leaving the building.

Kids' stuff? Overwrought imagination? Adolescent hysteria? According to Father Jeremy Davies of the Westminster Diocese, speaking in 2000, the incidence of demonic activity is rising. And whilst some who claim to be possessed by demons are fraudulent or require psychiatric rather than spiritual help, there are many who are sincerely in need of the aid of an exorcist.

The Revd Trevor Dearing was vicar of St Paul's, a small back-street parish church at Hainault. In a four year period from 1971 to 1975, he claimed to have driven out thousands of demons from the bodies of those who sought his aid.

'I don't go to them offering exorcism. They come to me asking

Trevor Dearing, vicar of St Paul's, Hainault, 1971–75.
(Trevor Dearing)

for it,' he said. 'They come and say, "I hear strange voices" or "I see frightening things" or "I feel I am being taken over by an evil spirit".'

Among his cases was 15 year old Margaret, a severely disturbed girl who had been unsuccessfully treated by psychiatrists over several years. Nothing that they tried could lift the burden of emotional disorder that Margaret carried. One evening she went to St Paul's with a friend and suddenly, during the service, she began screaming. Not without a struggle she was carried into the vestry where she smashed glass and furniture and attacked Dearing as he tried to control her. 'You have no power over me,' she yelled. 'I am stronger than you. Jesus died for you but he didn't die for spirits like me.'

Spirits like me? Whose voice was this? Was it really Margaret who claimed to be stronger than the vicar?

For several hours, the struggle, violently physical as well as mental and spiritual, continued in the vestry, Dearing supported throughout by four other members of the congregation. Finally, prayer as well as calm reasoning, prevailed.

'In the name of Jesus, go,' Dearing called out. 'Leave this girl.'

And at last Margaret was freed of the demons which for years had possessed her. She never again heard the voices which had urged her on in the past, voices which had determined her increasingly erratic behaviour. She was to become a regular church attender.

Another young woman who came to Trevor Dearing for help was Marlene, a good wife and mother, who quite suddenly had developed an intense sexual problem. When her husband was at work she began seeking men in town and taking them back to her home. She was disgusted with herself and yet seemingly incapable of controlling her behaviour. She felt guilty and dirtied by the whole change in her way of life. In deep despair she came to consult the vicar and yet as soon as she saw him she said: 'I am seduction' and this she went on repeating. Was it Marlene who made this boast? In the end the spirit which possessed her was successfully dismissed and Marlene restored to normality.

It ought to be emphasised that the Revd Dearing was extremely skilled at work of this nature. It takes training, experience, courage and belief to carry it out for the signs of demonic possession are terrifying not solely for the possessed but for those who encounter them. The afflicted at times have unexpected physical strength. On occasion, when they are confronted by religious objects, as they inevitably are when they are dealt with in churches, they are roused to ungovernable anger. But even in their own homes their families are often called on to face what appear to be total strangers whose facial expressions terrify them. In extreme cases they writhe like snakes on the floor and at other times their physical contortions seem almost to deny their human qualities. Sometimes their legs intertwine and no one can disentangle them. Yet others act like contortionists, their heads and feet touching the ground whilst the body arches. Some victims of demonic possession are known to levitate, raising themselves from their beds; their heads in extreme instances turning through 180 degrees. Sometimes they are lifted by some unseen force and thrown across the room. And there are the voice changes, the pitch, the tone, completely altered, as though someone else resided in the body.

Possession and the exorcism associated with it are accepted by most religions and beliefs. 'Heal the sick, raise the dead, cleanse lepers, cast out demons,' Christ said and the casting out of demons still has its place in the Christian Church.

As the Catholic Church, which has carried out many exorcisms in the United Kingdom in recent years, stated in 2000, 'Ever since apostolic times the Church has exercised the power she has received from Christ to cast out demons and demonic influence.' In its new rite of exorcism the Church no longer names the Devil as 'the Accursed Dragon, the Foul Spirit and the Enemy of Faith' but under whatever name, the enemy still shows himself. And in the year 2000, in the Vatican, Pope John Paul II himself carried out an exorcism of a girl who for years had been possessed.

Like all major religious groups the Catholic Church regulates each exorcism according to canon law, the priest requiring the authority of the bishop to carry out so delicate an operation. When the unskilled have dabbled in these matters there have been the most dreadful outcomes.

In 1974 in Yorkshire, for example, a devoted husband and father of five, who belonged to a small Christian Fellowship group, was deemed by other members to be possessed – his behaviour had been irrational and he had spoken in tongues – and he underwent an exorcism which lasted for several hours. He returned home and with his bare hands tore out his wife's eyes and tongue, ripping the flesh of her face almost from the bones. She ultimately choked on her own blood. There is no place for amateurish, well-meaning exorcism. It is dangerous. It is an encounter with evil.

And ignorance was at the root of the death by exorcism which occurred in Ilford in December 1993. In this case it concerned a loving and devout Muslim family and the outcome tore that family apart.

Twenty-two year old Farida Patel had for some months been troubled. In April 1993 she had gone to India for her traditionally arranged marriage. When, however, Farida's husband was refused an entry visa to the United Kingdom she returned home alone in September, hoping that he might be able to follow later. But Farida was deeply distressed by the separation and after her return home her irrational behaviour became increasingly worrying to her family. She spoke hysterically many times of the djinn (demon) who possessed her. He had threatened to cut out her tongue, she said, if she glorified Allah. For a girl whose faith was so strong this was terrifying.

The djinn, she would explain to the family, had been inside her since she was four years old and wished to marry her. The family, deeply alarmed, were quite convinced that Farida was possessed, especially when her behaviour was so terrifying. Sometimes she spoke to them in a man's voice or in the voice of an old person. At other times she assumed the posture of an old lady. On at least one occasion she claimed that the djinn pushed her. There was even some suggestion that she levitated, rising off the ground and hanging in mid-air. It was the djinn who made her behave so, of this the family were convinced. And so too was Farida, desperate for release from a condition which she herself recognised as possession.

In December 1993 the Patels reached a point of such desperation at their daughter's suffering that they sought help from the mosque, but there was no Imam available capable of dealing with the young woman's plight. But Mona Rai was on hand to take over and to advise them at this crucial point. Mohammed Patel, the father, had implicit faith in this educated 47 year old woman who lectured in mosques, schools and in private homes. In fact she was a regular visitor to the Patels' home where she instructed Farida and her sister, Rabiya, at 25 the mother of two small children, and their brother, 19 year old Hafiz, about the Koran and Islamic matters.

Mohammed Patel must have felt that Mona Rai, the woman known throughout the local Sunni Muslim community as 'The Teacher', was the ideal person to deal with his daughter's condition. If Farida was, as he suspected, possessed by a djinn, then this expert who had been teaching his children for the last two months about how the djinn were 'all around us and can harm us', was surely, in the absence of an Imam, the right person to attend to the affair. As for the revered Mona Rai, the guru, she had no doubt that Farida was possessed and that the djinn would have to be exorcised. She would attend to the matter, she said, aided by her disciple, Siraj Tutla, another friend of the Patels.

Farida, aware that the process would be demanding, was nevertheless desperate to be relieved of her agonies and, confident in the abilities of her teacher, she agreed that the exorcism should proceed. The whole procedure was to last over two days. It began on 9th December with prayers and readings from the Koran and throughout the time of the exorcism the prayers and readings continued. Mona Rai was confident, once Farida had indicated to her where exactly in her body the djinn was located, that she would overcome the enemy. At the outset she commanded it to leave by the girl's big toe. But all her commands and all her prayers had no discernible effect. Farida's demon still remained, stubbornly lodged inside her.

Such stubbornness, such a refusal to obey the holy words: Mona Rai introduced a new strategy. She used a plastic vacuum cleaner hose and beat the terrified young woman with it. This weapon and later a walking stick were used as were fists and feet over the two days. Indeed, Mona Rai, on the morning of the second day, before she went to the Patel household, spoke to some of her pupils at a London school about the exorcism. They had asked her how Farida could withstand such pain. Mona Rai had reassured them that in these circumstances Farida experienced no pain. It was the djinn who suffered, she told them.

Later Mona Rai set about her patient with a walking stick – the vacuum cleaner hose was broken – continuing until she was tired. She now handed over the task to Rabiya and Tutla who had been holding Farida down. Farida was screaming, shouting and weeping. Hafiz who came into the room was horrified at what he saw but Mona Rai challenged him at once.

'You're a man, the djinn is a man,' she said. 'Don't you want to help your sister?' She handed the stick to him and overcome by The Teacher's powerful personality and her formidable reputation, the boy hit his sister half a dozen times.

This remorseless attack went on hour after hour. Only when Farida started to vomit was there a pause in the proceedings. Mona Rai dismissed Mohammed Patel's anxious queries. Could they not pray, he asked, rather than use such violence on his child? And look at her face now, her yellow complexion. That was a good sign, Mona Rai told him, and when in tears the father expressed further doubt about the excessive force being used on his daughter, Mona Rai rounded on him.

'Don't you want your daughter to get better? She will have the djinn for life unless I beat it out of her,' she told the bewildered man. He too deferred to the superior knowledge of The Teacher.

All the while, in sessions each lasting five hours, the ferocious beating went on, accompanied by prayers and readings. Rabiya was to recall that from time to time Mona Rai referred to an instruction leaflet on exorcism. Eventually the walking stick broke and now Mona Rai jumped with her bare feet on the young woman's chest and stomach which is where she suspected the djinn still lurked.

The beating eventually stopped but not before Farida had been denied her last request for a glass of water. No, she was told, water might damage the progress of the exorcism.

Finally and unsurprisingly, after ten hours' beating, young Farida Patel died. 'Forgive me,' Mona Rai told the family, 'the djinn has taken her.'

Only then, it seems, did Mona Rai come to consider the seriousness of the situation. She and Siraj Tutla tried to persuade the family that Farida had been beating herself in the bedroom and had fallen, injured herself, and died from her injuries. Later she was to tell the police that she had never seen or taken part in any beatings. Tutla was to claim that all she had done was hold Farida's hand. It was Rabiya who was to blame, she said.

The inquest found that Farida died of multiple injuries, over one hundred, and she had nine broken ribs.

At their Old Bailey trial in November 1994, Rai, Tutla, and Hafiz Patel were charged with manslaughter. Tutla and Mona Rai faced the additional charge of trying to pervert the course of justice. Rabiya Patel pleaded guilty to unlawful killing of her sister. The prosecution accepted that this was not a case of murder. But the prosecution's principal point was that those taking part must have realised from her visible injuries and from her screams whenever she was hit that they were doing serious harm to Farida. And though it was accepted that in the earliest stages Farida had cooperated in the beatings, at the end the extent of her suffering must have been apparent.

Mona Rai, found guilty of the unlawful killing of Farida Patel, in what was described as a 'bizarre and barbaric' exorcism, was sentenced to seven years. She was branded as a fanatic and 'an arrogant charlatan'. Her confederate, Siraj Tutla, received three years while Rabiya and Hafiz Patel were each sentenced to one year's imprisonment. Hafiz's sentence was later reduced to three months.

Mr Ronald Thwaites for Rabiya Patel said: 'Mona Rai influenced this unfortunate family. They are the victims of the

Mona Rai arriving at court. (The Times)

worst form of cruelty and superstition which could be inflicted on trusting people by an arrogant charlatan who besmirches the name of an honourable religion in an attempt to exercise total control over others.'

After the trial, Bashir Choudry, who runs Ilford Muslim Centre and is Chairman of the League of British Muslims, warned people not to be conned by those 'posing as saviours.' It was easy for them to meddle in something they knew nothing about. His view was that Mona Rai and people like her preyed on the vulnerable. 'What Farida needed was to see a doctor because she was depressed at being separated from her husband.' He went on: 'This woman read a few books and then called herself a priestess. People should pray to their God if they are in trouble – you can do this alone or with your family without asking for outside help.'

Possession by demons is not far-fetched, is not simply the stuff of Hollywood. Most religious groups accept the notion of demons ready to attach themselves to humans. The clear lessons are, however, that there are dangers in dabbling with the supernatural. That way leads to madness, to death, to tragedy.

THE LAST WITCHMASTERS
OF CANEWDON

THEY say that James Murrell 'could do anything, cure anything and know anything, past, present and future.' It is a great claim to make but then great claims were regularly made for the men who with their knowledge of herbs were experts in natural medicine which they applied to men, women and ailing beasts. More than that, they could cast spells, could change fortunes and were in consequence much sought after. But the shoemaker, Cunning Murrell, was not just a run of the mill hedge-witch. He was far more powerful than that.

With his works about astrology and astronomy, conjuration and geomancy, with his books of spells and charms, of course he knew everything. Had he the mind to do so, he could paralyse with the Evil Eye. And they say that he could fly, that he could be in more than one place at once. He even forecast the date of his own death to the very day in 1860. There were few as powerful as Cunning Murrell, no more than five feet tall but possessor of a terrible authority for all that.

Though fearful of his skills, villagers would seek him out, would hear him respond to their knock at his door with his terrible cry: 'I am the Devil's Master.' But then, with the Devil's Master on their side, what had they to fear? They would go to him, these timorous village folk, with warts and lumps to be cured, with tales of sheep sickening and horses with the croup; with worries about this year's harvest. And there would be reluctant lovers to win over or perhaps bad neighbours to be taught a lesson. Sometimes there was property or crops to destroy, sometimes people.

Curses, they were a speciality of his and so was the lifting of curses. One wretched countryman cursed by another local witch went to Cunning Murrell. Follow the witch who has placed the evil on you, Murrell advised the man, and stick a knife into his footsteps. And everyone knows – or did know – that witches fear metal which is why locals used to put knives under their doormats. So the countryman followed the advice and the witch in agony lifted the curse.

From time to time Murrell's pre-eminence was challenged by other witches but no one matched him. Once, in a magical duel, when neither contestant seemed to be winning, Murrell summoned up all the elemental powers at his command and ordered his opponent to die. And so he did.

Murrell, though from Hadleigh, was the Master of the witches of Canewdon, that remote village on the marshland fringe, one of the last places in which the traditional belief in witches survived. Here until recent times children would dance seven times around the church to guard the village against witchcraft. Arthur Downes from the village, interviewed at the age of 94 in 1959, was asked if he had heard of Murrell. Of course he had. He recalled hearing a story in his youth about local people petitioning William Atkinson, the Vicar of Canewdon, 'to let Murrell exercise his whistling powers and make the witches confess themselves by dancing round in the churchyard.' Witchmasters who led local covens had this ability to summon up their priestesses. In this way, the villagers thought some witches who practised in secret would betray themselves.

But the Vicar refused to go ahead with this request because it is said that his own wife, Mary Ann, and her sister, Eliza, Lady Lodwick, were prominent in local witchcraft circles. They themselves would be called and unmasked.

One account had it that there would always be six witches in Canewdon, 'three in silk and three in cotton'. Cunning Murrell, on the other hand, had said: 'There will be witches in Leigh-on-Sea for 100 years and three in Hadleigh and nine in Canewdon for ever.' Whatever the number, the Vicar's wife and sister in law were presumably two of those 'in silk'. Arthur Downes thought there were more 'in silk' than 'in cotton' in Canewdon.

Accounts of witches in Essex go back to the earliest days of Christianity and its struggle to assert itself over the Old Religion of the Horned God. And while down the succeeding centuries great cathedrals and modest village churches were attended by the greater part of the population, there were many who hedged their bets and who kept the way open to the Old Gods and the men and women whom they regarded as guardians of the Old Ways.

There were periods when those who practised the old magic were hunted down. Witch trials in Chelmsford are recorded in 1566 and over the next hundred years there were over 1,200 witchcraft cases in the county. In the 1640s Manningtree's Matthew Hopkins, the Witchfinder General, a lawyer on the make, acting on behalf of Parliament, brought 200 before the courts of whom 68 were hanged or burned at the stake.

Even so, the Old Religion survived. Neither rope nor faggot could defeat it. And the likes of Cunning Murrell, priests of the Old Gods, continued to be sought after in rural Essex.

In the end, they say, Cunning Murrell was done for by witchcraft. A local man believed that Murrell had bewitched his donkey, bringing about its death. The aggrieved man put some of his donkey's hair into a bottle along with some of Murrell's and his own nail parings. He threw the bottle into the fire and it burst. Then came a loud banging at the door. The man ignored it. The next day Cunning Murrell was found dead.

Eric Maple, who investigated the folk traditions in Canewdon during the winter of 1959-1960, found that stories of past witchcraft still survived among farm folk. 'There is perhaps no other place in the British Isles where the belief in witchcraft survived so long and so late,' he wrote, 'and where legends of the old dark magic were told only a generation ago in the chimney corner. Little wonder that this district has always been known – and still is – as The Witch Country.'

Maple heard stories of the witches' meeting place at Canewdon crossroads, haunted by an executed witch; he was told of another spot, a barren patch of land down by the river in what is called the Witches Field, where witches met to renew their powers.

Another researcher, Clare Smythe, tells of how villagers in the 1950s could recall the witches of their childhood. One could inflict lice on her enemies; one could stop waggon wheels from turning; yet another had a glare so powerful that she could stop worshippers from entering church. These witches could turn and bend the forces of nature for good or evil. To what extent? Some spoke of death, of supernatural murder.

Most of all Maple and Smythe heard of Canewdon's most renowned witch, George Pickingill whose life, overlapping that of Cunning Murrell, spanned most of the 19th century and who died in his nineties in 1909 – or so they say. And such stories were told of him. Not that every researcher has been satisfied with them. Andrew Collins' recent work, for example, casts considerable doubt on Pickingill's powers though others have been convinced and the old man certainly has a place in the story of the witches of Essex.

'Old George' came from a line of Romany sorcerers, stretching back over many generations. A tall, rangy man, unkempt and generally incommunicative, he was sought out from time to time to perform white magic – to effect cures, to help with crops and animals, to find lost property. Seemingly greatly feared, he was believed by some to have sold his soul to the Devil. 'In Canewdon,' Eric Maple wrote, 'he was feared with an intensity that few modern people can understand.' So lest they should be bewitched the villagers deferred to him down the years.

Such powers the man was said to have. The Evil Eye – just one look and you were ill. And you wouldn't be well till he touched you with his blackthorn stick. Nor did he ever pay rent for his cottage up the lane by The Anchor. Neither beer nor clothing cost him a penny. Best not to get on the wrong side of 'Old George'. Stay away from him, that was best. Unless you had to, don't go near his place where at night the little red eyes of his familiars – in his case, white mice – could be seen glowing in the darkened cottage. Some said that if you had the nerve to look in the window, you might see 'Old George' in there, dancing, and all his familiars dancing with him, and all the furniture in the room and even the clock on the mantlepiece joining in. Such tales of the old fellow.

George Pickingill, in the tradition of many witches, apparently had the power to stop the farmers' machinery and at harvest time it is said that some farmers bribed him with beer to stay away. Small wonder that he ended the day dead drunk. He was an itinerant horse-dealer, unsurprising considering his Romany blood, but on occasion he would elect to do field work in harvest time. But, Maple was told, the wicked old chap would never do a hand's turn. Instead, he would sit in a field, smoking his pipe and drinking beer, whilst his familiars, his imps, the repositories of his power would mow it in double quick time. Or perhaps he simply sat in the field while anxious farmers were happy to pay him for doing nothing.

Even the local clergy were alleged to fear George Pickingill. At nights of the full moon and on the other festivals of the old world

Canewdon church c 1900.

and time, the coven would meet in St Nicholas' churchyard. Like Cunning Murrell before him, George Pickingill was said to blow on his wooden whistle to summon his witches, all of them women. Inevitably there was some noise, of chanting, of prayers; there was ritual sex magic and ceremonial; there were flames and dancing. And in the vicarage, the old incumbent would sit, afraid to confront whoever, whatever, danced in his churchyard.

And then a new man came to the church, unwilling to permit the licence, the paganism, the offence to his religion. When he heard the noise, the chants, the alien prayers, out he went into the churchyard, armed with a riding crop, making his way through the shadows, to put an end to it all. But all was silent. There was no movement. No sounds, no fires. All was still. And all the puzzled clergyman could see were 13 white rabbits, half-hidden by the gravestones. The ability to transform oneself into another creature – that is, to shapeshift – is what witches of any substance were always said to be able to do.

Presumably there were other sites, sacred to the witches, where Pickingill's covens met to conduct their rituals under the full moon, naked, with him as the priest, along with the priestesses of the coven, worshipping the Mother Goddess. How many others attended, not witches but merely adherents, believers in the Old Religion?

George Pickingill, Witchmaster of Canewdon, is a significant

George Pickingill, the last wizard of Canewdon.

figure in the history of modern witchcraft. According to some investigators, the old countryman was called upon to demonstrate his magic – perhaps his link with Satan – to scholars, intellectuals, wealthy middle and upper class people, landowners and the like, who were also involved in the dark and secret world of magic and witchcraft. When all these clever folk asked him the most abstruse questions about the occult arts, did he really reply with automatic writing and was he aided in this by a spirit guide? Could he really leave his body at will? It is claimed that even Aleister Crowley, 'The Great Beast', 'The Worst Man in the World', consulted him as an authority on matters of witchcraft, as did other black magicians. Certainly 'Old George' has been labelled, not solely by Eric Maple, as 'the last and perhaps greatest of the (Essex) wizards', but by others as 'England's most notorious witch.'

Yet it is odd that there is such a mystery attached to his death. Read the books and you find that Pickingill died in 1909 at the age of 93, or perhaps 105. (So much, by the way, for a man who allegedly had the secret of eternal life!) And there are stories about that death. Just shows how legends grow, how myths attach themselves to certain figures. For instance, in one account, on the night before his death the old man was drinking in The Anchor, no doubt knocking back the free ale that he had enjoyed for most of his days. Suddenly, there was a clap of thunder and a flash of lightning. Then George Pickingill's cottage took fire. An omen? And is it true?

One story has him in hospital on the day of his death, a worn skeletal figure, recognised by a witness who described seeing his familiars, those white mice of his, sucking his nipples.

There is another version of what occurred on the day he died. Apparently 'Old George' was fit enough to be out and about in the village on a raw, dull day, when a gust of wind blew his hat over the churchyard wall. The old man climbed over to retrieve it but as he did so, the sun came out unexpectedly. The shadow of a cross on a headstone suddenly fell across his face and the witch fell to the ground, cursing God and the Church with his dying breath. A neat enough story, a fitting end one might think for one whose purpose in life had been to oppose the Christian Church. But life, and death for that matter, is rarely so cleverly sculpted. Part of the legend one might think.

Yet another story tells how 'Old George' had promised that something memorable would occur at his funeral. When the hearse drew up at the church, the horses, unaided, stepped out of the shafts and galloped off. A message from beyond?

The trouble with this is that there must be some very great doubt about George Pickingill being accepted for burial at St Nicholas' church. He who had danced there with his coven; he who had terrified not only his fellow villagers but the clergy too; he who had conducted what amounted to sex orgies in the churchyard; he who had cursed the church and he whose Master was allegedly Satan – could there have been any chance at all of his being buried in hallowed ground? Or if he was buried there, does this suggest that perhaps his reputation has been somewhat overstretched? And it has to be admitted that his obituary makes no mention of his remarkable powers.

So who was it they buried at St Nicholas' church on 14th April 1909? Was it someone else? Was it the old man's son, another George, who did not share his father's reputation? Possibly. Or perhaps it was another man of the same name, a common enough surname in those parts, another aged Romany, a horse whisperer, they say. Was there some confusion in the memory of those who were consulted by Eric Maple all those years later?

And so where does that leave 'Old George'? Possibly in some unmarked, unhallowed spot. But when did he die? In the first few years of the 20th century, certainly, but it may not be possible to guess more accurately than that.

A mystery, certainly. As is his reputation in the eyes of some researchers. Was George Pickingill one of the greatest witches? Or was he simply an old countryman, a typical Cunning Man with a gift, with the capacity to effect a few impressive cures? And did he, as the years went on, collect about him a wholly unmerited fame, the product of fireside tales, rumours, imagination, village gossip? Were some researchers gulled by locals into the creation of a myth? Or did George Pickingill truly deserve to be known as 'England's most notorious witch'?

GUILTY BUT ASLEEP

IT was a lorry driver who found her, that raw, third day of January in 1961. He had pulled in at the Oaker Hill lay-by, just outside Ridgewell on the A604, the Cambridge-Colchester road. He had jumped down from the cab, not intending to hang around on such a bitter morning. All he wanted to do was answer a call of nature so he'd slipped a few yards into the field and it was there he saw her.

The girl was lying face downwards in a ditch. Her head was partly submerged; her arms and manicured fingers trailed in the freezing water, swollen by winter floods. It was a lonely spot, a grim place in such bitter weather. And he could see that the scantily dressed corpse was partly frozen, the ice formed on it. Over her, a blackberry bush seemed to offer some kind of bleak cover.

She wore a white blouse, a black bra, a tight fitting black skirt and a single red garter. But she wore neither shoes nor stockings. Nor was there any sign of outdoor clothing. Odd in this harsh season, the morning cold and hard as iron. Nor, when they were called to the crime scene, could the police find a handbag. And the labels had been cut out of what clothing she was wearing. Even more curious, her hair had been cropped until it resembled a crew cut. It was crudely done, as though someone had roughly seized hold of the hair at the front of the head and chopped away at random.

The police surgeon, called to the site, estimated that she had been dead for perhaps a couple of days. She had been strangled. On New Year's Eve or New Year's Day, perhaps, though no one had called the police with any missing person enquiry. All that the detectives were certain of was that she had been carried to where she lay for there were no spots of mud on her feet and legs. And the absence of outdoor clothing hinted that she had been murdered inside, some place where presumably she had left her clothing.

Within hours the police had a name for the victim. Jean Constable, a 20 year old Halstead girl who worked in the local plastics factory, had not returned home from the New Year's Eve party she had told her parents she was going to. She had been looking forward to it. Jean was a party girl, a cheerful soul, described as being fond of men and particularly of the GIs from the base at Wethersfield. She and a few other girls had planned to go up to Holland Park with some American soldiers.

When Jean did not come home on New Year's Day, a Sunday, her mother and father were not at all surprised. She liked to enjoy herself. Jean was a good girl, her parents and her friends would always say. Good and lively, she enjoyed herself and why not, she was young. And even though they had always told her to be careful, they had been confident that she could look after herself. That is why they did not raise the alarm when she didn't turn up on the Monday or even the Tuesday. She'd be staying with friends, they assumed. She often did. But not this New Year.

The Constables were surprised to learn that their daughter had not been up to London for the New Year's party. They knew she had planned to go with some American soldiers but they were not sure of their names. They were able, however, to give the names of other GIs known to Jean though whether these were the ones who had intended going to Holland Park they could not say.

So why did Jean Constable not go to the party in London which she had so much looked forward to? Easily solved, as it turned out. She did not turn up in time and the others went off without her. But where was she? Easy again, because many people had seen her on New Year's Eve. She was visiting the pubs in Braintree, partying with her usual enthusiasm.

Several people had seen her quite early in the evening at the Nag's Head in Braintree. She had met a young man there, a civilian, not an American. Later some saw her in the company of a GI who seemed angry about something. They surmised that Jean must have been flirting with someone else at the time. No wonder he was annoyed, they had thought, and him just like a film star, very tall and very handsome. Although in the next couple of days the police were to seek the tall and handsome American they never found him. Or if they did, he was dismissed from their enquiries very soon.

Then there were reports of Jean moving on to another of her favourite haunts, the Bell, drinking and dancing and having a generally good time as she always did in the pubs frequented by the GIs. And even if it wasn't London, the Bell knew how to put on a good New Year's Eve party. At one stage she was pressing some of the girls there to come with her to another party at the nearby US Air Force base at Wethersfield but all of these suggestions were turned down. Everybody had their plans made. Still, even if her trip to London had fallen through and no-one was up for the base, Jean seemed happy enough. She had the young English civilian with her and she had enough partners to dance with and to keep filling her glass.

And in the noise and the music and the excitement she met an American, a man she already knew. Would she come back with him to his flat, he asked her? Have a little party of their own? Yes, fine, she could bring the civilian along if she wanted. She'd been with him all evening after all. It wasn't right to desert him now. Witnesses saw her leave the Bell before midnight in the company of two men. One of them, the American, was known as 'Bill' but no one knew his surname. All three were pretty drunk according to those who saw them leave.

Teams of police were now despatched to the Wethersfield base which housed the 20th Tactical Fighter Wing of the United States Air Force. Here there were over 2,000 airmen and their families, stationed at one of the biggest US fighter stations in Britain. Over the next 24 hours the police questioned hundreds of men – Alabamans and Texans, New Englanders and Kentuckians, men from every city and state. They spoke to pilots and electricians, flight mechanics and clerks, officers and enlisted men. The number needing to be seen was formidable. And there was such a range of uncertain, ill-remembered tales from New Year's Eve to query, to check.

And at last, after long hours, they came across Willis Eugene Boshears, a 29 year old staff sergeant with a distinguished service career going back eleven years. He was working as ground staff, as an engineer, but in Korea he had flown 49 missions as a rear gunner and had been twice decorated for bravery. A slightly built man, with pale blue eyes and a thin face, he was softly spoken and when the detectives asked if they might speak to him he betrayed no signs of anxiety.

Over several hours of questioning, Boshears explained that he was living in a flat in Great Dunmow and that his 23 year old wife was away visiting her parents in Scotland, letting them see the latest born of their three children. He would have joined her in Scotland for Hogmanay, Boshears told the detectives, but he had been required to remain on duty. He volunteered other basic facts about his life, too. Yes, he was known as 'Bill' and to the police this was interesting, for hadn't Jean Constable been in the company of a 'Bill' when she left the Bell?

Boshears told how he had started drinking early on the morning of 31st December. It was a Saturday and he was not required for duty. He had gone from Great Dunmow to the base where he had drawn his pay. After breakfasting at the NCOs club, he started with a couple of vodka aperitifs and followed those up with a couple of vodka chasers. The remainder of the morning he spent drinking and had then left the base with a large bottle of 100 per cent proof vodka. On the way home he had called in at the pub at Great Bardfield and here he'd had a couple of pints. At his flat he had more drink and then he had gone to Braintree, visiting first the Bell, then the Boar and then he had returned once more to the Bell where there was a lively party. Here he admitted to having met Jean Constable, whom he already knew, and her companion, the 20 year old man, but he explained that he had left them in the Bell and had gone home to Great Dunmow.

Only after hours of persistent probing did Boshears finally admit that Jean had gone back to Great Dunmow with him. But the young man, the chap who came from Leicester, he thought, had accompanied them. In the flat they had continued drinking and dancing, the three of them. He had put on the record player which the people in the flat below, another US service couple, had complained about. They had had to turn down the volume. Boshears admitted that they had been very noisy but then it was New Year.

Then the detectives questioning him heard Boshears' astonishing account of what had occurred, and this was the version of the happenings of early New Year's Day that he was to stick by. Part of what Boshears said was confirmed by the mysterious young man, David Salt, a 20 year old engineer from Leicester, who, having read of Jean's death, surrendered himself to the police. He was anxious that he should not be accused of the crime. As it was, Salt's innocence was soon established and his sole importance to the case is that his account tallies with Boshears', up to the point when he left the flat. Jean Constable was alive then, Salt told the police. At about 12.45 am he had asked Jean if she wanted a lift home but she had said she was too tired to leave and just wished to sleep, so he had left.

Boshears claimed that he had gone into the bedroom while David Salt and Jean had intercourse. He had brought a mattress from the bedroom and put it in front of the fire. Whether they had had more drinks and whether they had danced again is unclear. Boshears' and Salt's accounts are less than specific about time and the order of events but they agree that at some point all three had lain on the mattress. Boshears had fallen asleep.

'The next thing I remember is someone scratching at my face,' Boshears told both police and court. 'I opened my eyes. She was lying there under me and I had my hands around her throat. Then I realized she was dead. I'd been very drunk but that sobered me a little.'

He was alone in the house now, his mind in a whirl. He had carried Jean's naked body into the spare bedroom and locked the door.

'Then I went back to the mattress and lay down again, trying to think what to do. But I fell asleep. . . When I woke up in the morning I decided that the whole thing was a bad dream. But then I looked in the spare bedroom. There was Jean, and she was dead. I was so panic-stricken that I nearly dropped dead myself.'

Later he took the body into the bathroom, washing it and then dressing it in the way in which it was later found. He had taken the sheets and blankets off the bed on which the young girl had lain and put them in the bath tub to wash away any stains. For two days, from early on the Sunday until after 11 o'clock on the Monday, he had left the body in the spare room. When he was sure that it was safe to do so he had put it in the back of the car and had driven it to Ridgewell where he had dumped it in a ditch. He had hoped in some forlorn way to make identification difficult and for this reason he had cut Jean's hair and had taken all of the manufacturer's labels out of her clothing. But it was a quite hopeless stratagem.

Having got rid of the body he had returned home and burned all of the other items belonging to the girl: the grey and black fur coat, the handbag, the stockings, the suspender belt, the black gaberdine jacket with the white collar, the black high-heeled winkle-picker shoes and one red garter.

He threw away her ring and her gold wrist watch as they might have been recognised but, somewhat meanly it seems, he had kept a ten shilling note from her handbag.

Throughout the succeeding weeks and at his two-day trial at the Assizes at Chelmsford which began on 17th February, Boshears was to claim that he had no memory of what had occurred. 'I don't know how it all came about. I don't know what happened,' he would say. He swore that there had been no quarrel with the girl nor had he made any overtures after Salt left. He was too drunk and sleepy for any kind of activity. He did not dispute his responsibility for the girl's death. He had killed her and he would not deny it. But, he maintained, it was not a conscious act. This was the nub of his defence. The charge was murder but the sergeant's defence was that as he had strangled Jean Constable in his sleep, no crime had been committed. His counsel submitted that this was a clear case of automatism, indicating that Boshears had been sleeping so soundly when he strangled Jean that he could not be held accountable for his actions.

Mr Stanley Rees QC for the prosecution contended that Boshears had murdered Jean, perhaps when she repulsed him after Salt's departure. Salt himself had been of the view that Boshears was anxious for him to leave and he drew his own conclusions as to the reason. In fact he did not think that Boshears was as drunk that night as he was now claiming to be. Salt also felt that Jean, although she said that she wanted to stay on because she was tired, had other things in her mind too.

Mrs Clara Miller, the neighbour, whose husband had earlier complained about the noise from the record player, testified to hearing someone crying or sobbing at about 1 o'clock. She had heard a female call out either 'You love me', or 'You don't love me.'

Mr Rees was to suggest that Boshears, though drunk, was very much aware of what was happening. Salt and Jean had twice had intercourse in his flat, in his presence. The prosecution contended that this was enough to inflame the American's passions. It had all led to the girl's death.

Mr Gerald Hines for the defence was to concede in part what the defence was saying. 'To say the atmosphere in the flat was erotic and that there was a good deal of inflamed passion is obvious,' Hines said. But Boshears, his counsel insisted, though he might have been willing, was certainly too drunk to take part in any romps with Jean.

This extraordinary though not unique plea did not go unchallenged. Even the judge, Mr Justice Glyn-Jones, made plain his mistrust of such a defence.

When the Home Office pathologist, Professor Francis Camps, was in the witness box, he expressed the opinion that Boshears would probably have felt the girl moving as he strangled her, even if he was half asleep. This would have been enough to waken him up. Probably.

Judge: He could not possibly have carried this through without waking up?

Camps: I should think that it is certainly within the bounds of improbability. My reason, from my findings, is this process would take a certain amount of time, and during that the person would go through certain phases of movement, and from the description given of finding her suddenly dead like that I don't think it fits in with that type of death.

But Professor Camps was forced to concede that such a killing was not impossible.

In summing up, the judge asked: 'Have you ever heard of a man strangling a woman while he was sound asleep? We have no medical evidence that there exists any record in all the records of the medical profession that such a thing ever happened. . . you use your common sense and decide whether it happened.'

The judge instructed the jury that if they believed that Boshears had been asleep and committed the act involuntarily he was entitled to be acquitted. If there were any doubts about whether he was asleep or not then he must be given the benefit of that doubt and acquitted. Only if they rejected the defence could they convict. There were only two possible verdicts in the case, the judge said: guilty of murder or not guilty of anything at all.

After nearly two hours the jury returned a verdict of not guilty. Tony Johnson, one of the detective sergeants who had interrogated the American, was galled when Boshears walked up to him as the court cleared and said: 'Gee, Mr Johnson, I think your British justice is just wonderful.' Was Boshears crowing? Had he pulled a fast one as Johnson seemed to think?

In July 1961, having returned to America with his loyal wife, Boshears was discharged 'under less than honourable conditions.' from the Air Force he had served with such distinction. The American authorities clearly shared Dr Camps' scepticism about people who claimed they had killed in their sleep. The US military

Staff Sgt Willis Eugene Boshears, tried for the murder of Jean Constable.
(Daily Express)

had at the outset attempted to have Boshears tried by Court Martial rather than in an English court but that had been refused. But they made clear by their subsequent action what they felt about the verdict of a foreign court.

And would the Americans have reached any different conclusion from the jury at Chelmsford? There is in fact distinct doubt about how other British juries would have responded. Despite the judge's implication that such a case was unknown, there have been other instances of killing while asleep.

In Glasgow in 1878, a man said to be subject to violent nightmares killed his baby son in his sleep. The jury said that due to his state of somnambulism the man had not been responsible for his actions. He was acquitted.

In 1946, however, a sailor was found guilty of a so-called sleep-walk murder in London and was executed.

Only five years later, a naval officer in Plymouth was charged with the attempted murder of his wife during sleep. The man was acquitted.

All three cases were tried before the Boshears case and only serve to suggest that this is an especially difficult kind of offence to bring to court. More recently, in 1998, a Devon man murdered his wife with a knife and hammer. He had been drunk when he went to bed. The man was remorseful, pleading that he did not know what he was doing. He was given life imprisonment.

After the Boshears case Lord Elgin asked in the Lords whether the government had plans to make a change in the law to make possible a verdict of Guilty but Asleep which would effectively prevent a similar defendant from walking free from punishment. It was obvious where his sentiments lay.

But how differently it might all have turned out. Supposing Jean had arrived in time for the jaunt up to Holland Park? Or what if she had found someone to go to the Wethersfield base party with her? What if Boshears had not been required to be on duty over the New Year and instead had been free to travel to Scotland to be with his wife and her family? How different the lives of so many could have been.

Willis Eugene Boshears was killed in a car crash in the USA some years later. Some say it was suicide.

A bad end to a sad tale.

THE AVELEY ENCOUNTER

JUST passed through Hornchurch. Not much traffic on the road. Very quiet for a Sunday night. And just as well because John was anxious to get home by 10.30 pm. There was a play on BBC2, *The Girls in their Summer Dresses*, and he was hoping to see it but they'd stayed so long at Sue's parents at Harold Hill that it was all a rush. Still, they were nearing home now. They'd be in Aveley in a few minutes. All they'd have to do was put the kids to bed. Eight year old Karen was already asleep in the back along with Stuart aged three. But Kevin was still awake, talking away, taking no notice of the chat show on local radio.

Kevin was occupied with the blue star, kept drawing his father's attention to it. It looked no more than 500 yards away and seemed to be keeping pace with them but stopping and starting from time to time. A helicopter? A passenger plane? No. More like a UFO, Kevin? What about that, eh? Funny, it was oval-shaped, quite unusual.

Just outside Aveley, as they were rounding the bend in the road, it struck them that there was no sound from the engine, nor was there any road noise. And then the radio began to splutter and smoke. What was wrong with it? Was it going to short circuit? John reached down and jerked out the wires. And then quite unexpectedly saw the mist in front of them, right across the road, and high, eight or nine feet. And green. He had no time to brake though he did notice the immediate fall in temperature. Then they were into the mist with a jolt . . . and out of it with yet another jolt.

During the remaining few hundred yards to their home both John and Sue Day felt unaccountably unsettled. Something uncanny, something disturbing, seemed to have occurred but they were unable to define what it was. When they reached their house, while John replaced the car wiring, Sue put the children to bed and then went downstairs to switch on the television. But BBC2 was blank. Nor was there any response from the other channels. How strange. What could have happened? She looked at her watch. It showed one o'clock. Nonsense. They'd just come in. They'd left Harold Hill only half an hour or so earlier. She looked at the clock. Same story. One o'clock. Madness. Puzzled she rang TIM. The time was one o'clock.

On Sunday, 27th October 1974, the Day family lost nearly three hours.

In the succeeding months and years there were some changes in the Day household. Sue went back to college to improve her qualifications. Kevin, who was designated a backward reader in school, suddenly and unaccountably put a spurt on and quite surpassed others in his class with his reading skills. And John, who had had many different jobs working as a joiner since leaving school, decided that he wanted to work with the mentally handicapped.

And there were other changes too. All of the family with the exception of Stuart turned against meat-eating. John and Sue found themselves nauseated by the smell of cooked meat and they were now against the killing of animals for food on principle. They gave up alcohol and John, a one-time heavy smoker, forswore tobacco. They were more and more inclined towards healthy eating.

But there was a down side. Shortly after their odd experience in the mist John had a nervous breakdown and it was some months before he took up his new work with the mentally handicapped. And they all began to suffer nightmares. And then there was an outbreak of poltergeist activity when articles would disappear for days only to reappear in some strange location. There were unaccountable tappings and clickings in the house. On occasion the Days' bedroom was pervaded with the scent of lavender whilst at other times there was a sickly sweet smell. Sometimes it seemed that an airplane hovered just over the roof. One evening, the Days saw their television rise three inches in the air. One night when Andrew Collins, who wrote an authoritative account of what came to be called 'The Aveley Encounter', stayed with the Days, he heard loud crashing sounds in the kitchen. Then he was overcome by a soothing sensation which left him feeling peaceful. This is jam-packed with much of the illogicality of a poltergeist infestation. Was it a consequence of some unsuspected traumatic

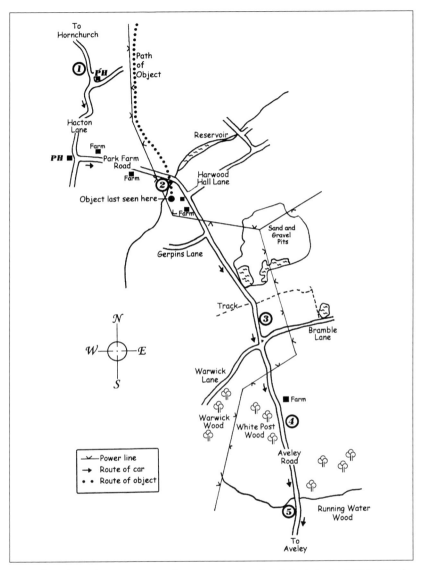

Map detailing the sequence of events on that fateful night in 1974: (1) the light in the sky first seen (2) the light last seen passing to the right in front of the car (3) green mist appeared here (4) John Day's first recall of their whereabouts after encountering the mist (5) Sue Day's first recall of their whereabouts after encountering the mist.

disturbance that some member of the family had been subject to?

In a local newspaper an article about UFOs, written by Andrew Collins, had interested John. He wondered if perhaps the explanation of their curious experience in the mist and the time-loss lay in Ufology. His initial efforts to get in touch with the local UFO group were unsuccessful but eventually Collins heard about the family at Aveley and contacted them in the summer of 1977. From August to December 1977 there was a series of interviews and three sessions of regression hypnosis which produced Collins's astonishing report which was published in Volumes 23 and 24 of *Flying Saucer Review*. Collins did much of the interviewing and Dr Leonard Wilder was responsible for the hypnosis sessions which took place at the home of Dr Bernard Finch. At times Jenny Randles, the writer and eminent paranormal investigator, was present.

Both John and Sue had had terrifying nightmares in the last three years and there was a recurrent dream in which a deep red sun hung in a blood red sky. Below, in a devastated landscape lines of defeated people found their way to the top of a hill. It was an image of Armageddon. On the hilltop the people waited and then from over the horizon came spaceships to rescue them. It was as if an elite had been selected to be saved from the dying Earth. When shown photographs both John and Sue identified Dragon Hill at Uffington in Berkshire, a location potent in myth, as the site of their dream. What could it signify?

The Days would not permit Kevin, ten years old by the time of the investigation, to undergo hypnosis but they were very willing to discover what might be the root of their own difficulties and if it lay in their curious experience. Under hypnosis, they were taken back to childhood and spoke in childish voices. When John was asked to regress to another life he revealed himself as a 17th century ploughman, Jim Dayliss, and on this occasion he spoke in rustic tones and used strange turns of phrase and vocabulary.

John's memory of 27th October 1974 went as far as driving into the mist and driving out again. Under hypnosis, John offered the following description of what occurred during the missing three hours. He recalled that as he went towards the green mist there was also a strong beam of white light. The light enveloped the car and he described the sensation of the car being raised in the beam. Then he found himself on a balcony of a hangar. He was looking down at a blue car; it was not his own white Vauxhall

Victor Estate but he saw the driver slumped over the steering wheel and a sleeping woman next to him. On the rear seat were three other recumbent figures. He had the notion that he was looking at himself, his wife and children. It was like an out-of-body experience. By his side were Sue and Kevin. Behind John was a figure, 6'8" tall, wearing a seamless suit. The figure, the man, the entity wore a kind of tight fitting hood and the lower part of his face was covered. And he had three fingers on each hand.

Without any resistance John went off with his guide, walking towards a wall which had no door. But somehow as they approached a door opened. On this craft it seems there were instant doors. They entered another room. Like all of the rooms John went into it was oval-shaped. It was like being on the inside of a bubble. There was a table here above which hung lights. These were the only lights he saw on the craft. In all of the other spaces the light seemed to emanate from the uniformly grey walls.

And under hypnosis John continues to tell what happened. The tall figure touches John and he loses consciousness and wakes to find himself on the table. There are three tall figures now and beside them two small creatures, ugly and frightening, neither more than 4 feet tall. They are slightly hunched and have bushy hair over their heads and hands. Unlike the tall, three-fingered entities, these creatures have four fingers with long talons. It is these who appear to be conducting a physical examination, passing what John believes to be a scanner over him and later exploring his body with a 'pen'. These examiners are skilled at what they do, that much is evident, but they are clearly subservient to the tall figures.

John is then taken on a tour of the spacecraft. He has worked out that the hangar area with the balcony is the lower tier. The examination room is on the middle tier and here, linked by passageways, are a laboratory and leisure and rest rooms. On the top tier is the control room. Here he is shown maps, pictures, diagrams in rapid succession and finally he sees a hologram. This shows, John is told, what the planet these aliens once occupied looked like in its last years. They had ruined it, destroyed it by pollution and other reckless treatment of their environment. They had had two suns and had destroyed them through their arrogant wastefulness; they had lost one of their moons by their misuse of their resources. There is a message here, a warning, for John Day.

But they will not say where they come from. John has heard the word 'Phobos' mentioned but it has no significance for him. He is unaware that Phobos is the smallest satellite of Pluto. He has the idea now that these aliens have several bases deep under the seas but they are reluctant to discuss this.

And now, he is told, it is time for him to leave . . . and the car jolts and judders and he drives out of the mist. The road is clear and he remembers that he will have to repair the car radio before he goes in to see the TV play . . .

Sue's recollections under hypnosis are in many ways similar to her husband's. The mist, the white pillar of light, the car rising, being on the balcony looking down at the blue car . . . but when Kevin is led away she is much more frightened. She struggles when they take her to the examining room. She remembers how the examiners, the ugly little creatures, explored her body with the 'pen' and their particular interest in her left side, especially the area of the kidneys.

Sue recalls going to the control room; the entity who strummed music out of the empty air; being told that they did not, could not procreate. 'We produce through you,' she was told. 'You are our children.' As though they looked over us, looked out for us.

Sue's experience also ended in the control room but she saw John and the children drive off, away from the spacecraft, into and out of the mist. John's first recollection is of driving past White Post Wood. Sue cannot recall anything until she was passing Running Water Woods half a mile further on . . . and home was only a few hundred yards away and she would have to put the kids to bed while John repaired the car radio . . .

So what are we to make of this? This is the first reported British case of alien abduction. And it is about people who have been condemned as cranks and fantasists, as outright liars. It is easy enough to dismiss such claims. But there are many such cases which have been investigated and whilst a considerable number has been rejected as fraudulent, others have the smack of conviction about them. And the Days do not seem like sensation seekers. Would they wait for three years before telling their story? Why make it so elaborate a tale? Why invent the beaming up into the machine? It would have been easier to sustain a story of being met outside the craft. And why the radical change of lifestyle?

There are several cases of alien abduction involving cars on lonely roads at night, of their being teleported with their occupants into a spaceship. Has this environment, the dark, the enclosed space, the hum of the engines, the sound of tyres some hypnotic effect? Where it causes some drivers to doze off, do others experience something else?

And it may surely be argued that if we can travel to the Moon and Mars, to Jupiter and Venus, others, older than we, more advanced than we, may have already beaten us to it. What if they have conquered space and even time and now see it as some kind of mission to save us from the very faults that led to their disaster?

Some argue that there are conscious non-physical intelligences which take on specific shapes that the viewer can understand. So, therefore, are there intelligences which wished for some obscure reason to pass on a message to humanity through the Days? And did these intelligences take on the kind of shapes – bodies, spaceship – that made some recognisable sense to them?

Or is there a curious capacity which allows some people to be exposed in certain circumstances to inexplicable psychic drama? Perhaps such a capacity would be, to a heightened degree, what in children we might call a hyperactive imagination but which might better be described as a powerful and creative subconscious. It may be that John Day, who as a child had twice seen apparitions and to whom UFOs had appeared on other occasions, has that heightened imaginative capacity, some creative, subconscious drive? Does he, perhaps with unsuspected mediumistic powers, almost act as a magnet to paranormal elements? But then it does take some explaining why, if this were the case, Sue Day was a participant in the Aveley encounter. Still, there is ample evidence of multiple hallucinations. But then, what about the time-lapse?

There is a vast literature on this subject which as yet is not totally respectable in the scientific world. The authoritative Jenny Randles, convinced at the time that the Days had been abducted, now believes that other paranormal factors – a 'time-storm', she suggests – had come in to play. The regression hypnosis, she feels, might have created some kind of fantasy in the minds of the Days. But the whole business is mightily baffling and well worth pondering. Are we really sure what is out there?

THE WITCH OF
SCRAPFAGGOT GREEN

'QUEER things are happening in the remote Essex village of Great Leighs, strange things that seem to defy any normal explanation. Along the straggling lanes and among its scattered cottages, the villagers will tell you great stones are moved mysteriously, straw ricks are overturned on windless nights, sheep stray through unbroken hedges, church bells ring at odd hours. And the eerie centre of it all is Scrapfaggot Green, a spot that might have been named by the witch herself.'

This is St John Cooper, ace reporter of the now defunct *Sunday Pictorial*, writing of his visit to Essex in the issue of 6th October 1944 under the banner headline: WITCH WALKS AT SCRAPFAGGOT GREEN. To this reporter down from London a witch, long dead now, is responsible for such strange goings-on.

Of course, says the reporter, the locals have no doubt that the witch is at the root of the trouble. Old Agnes Haven had been burned at the stake, so the story went, and buried at the very site of her death on Scrapfaggot Green where the three roads meet at the end of Drakes Lane. A great stone had been placed over her all those years ago. That would keep her down.

And presumably it did its work until the Americans came. In 1943 the Americans demolished Duke's Wood for a new airfield and widened local roads for their great military vehicles. And in the widening of Drakes Lane they just threw the old witch's stone into a ditch. Can you wonder at what happened after that?

According to St John Cooper, nearly everyone has a story to tell about things that don't tally with common sense. They almost queue up to talk to him. Councillor Arthur Sykes has his say: 'Every day I hear of new mischief in the village. Alf Quilter the shepherd will tell you of sheep straying from his fields where there is not a hurdle out of place or a hole in his hedges big enough for a rabbit to run through. People have told me of hearing the church bells being rung at midnight. Yesterday the old church clock was found to be two hours slow and I don't remember it being wrong before.'

Anxious to persuade his readers of the impeccable quality of his witness, St John Cooper tells them that Councillor Sykes is 'no superstitious Essex man.' In other words, he is not a dull-witted yokel. No, the councillor is 'a hard-headed Lancashire man', a fact that ought to clinch his evidence. And the hard-headed Sykes goes on to say, 'No, I don't believe in witches – but I've got to admit there have been strange happenings here since that old stone was shifted.'

Sykes tells the reporter that he had bought three geese to fatten up for Christmas. He had just received them that very morning. 'We walked to the back garden to see them. They were gone. There was no sign of a feather, no break in their enclosure.' The old witch about her business?

Next St John Cooper went off to interview the local builder, Charlie Dickson. He was having some trouble too. The scaffolding poles which he kept overnight in his yard had just been scattered about like matchsticks. And they were heavy. Some supernatural force, eh?

There was more, Dickson confided. He took the *Pictorial* man to a small cottage behind the Dog and Gun. The night before, when the painters had knocked off work at the cottage, they had left their equipment neatly stacked up. And where was it now? There wasn't a sign of it. Only after diligent searching of the cottage did they find in the attic their dozen paint pots. They were heavy paint pots, too, according to St John Cooper, as if superhuman strength had been required to take them upstairs.

'You see,' Charlie Dickson told the reporter, 'this is the kind of thing that's always happening. It's meaningless. Yesterday we found a dead chicken in the water butt – a chicken with its neck twisted. Yet nobody has missed one in the district.' And the case of the missing chicken was never resolved.

In the face of such threatening supernatural activity, St John Cooper took the only action open to a hardened newspaperman. 'We went,' he confides, 'to the Dog and Gun to soothe our nerves.' But even there, there was no escape from the frightening paranormal occurrences.

At first Bill Reynolds, the landlord, had scoffed at all the daft tales. His wife had heard sounds in the night, he said, but he had always thought mice were responsible.

Only when they made to leave the Dog and Gun, however, was the landlord to change his mind for there was a huge stone not five feet from the front door.

'Somebody's going to break their necks over that one night,' said Charlie Dickson.

'Over what?' said the landlord. He stood staring at the stone. 'Where did that come from?' he said. 'That wasn't there before.' Another inexplicable paranormal happening?

It took two of them to remove the stone. It had not been long there, that much was certain. St John Cooper observed that there was no sign of damp below. 'I cannot explain how that stone got there without the landlord or one of the cottagers knowing,' he wrote. 'It would have taken three men to move it far.'

Next it was the turn of Ernest Withen of Chadwicks Farm to present his evidence of supernatural interference. The waggons in his barn had been turned round in the night and it had taken the men half an hour to get them out this morning. Furthermore, his newly built haystacks had tumbled down in the night. And there had been no wind. What could it all mean? What was to be done? There were so many queer, nonsensical, meaningless things happening day after day.

'That witch, proper mischief-like, she be,' say the villagers, articulating their view to the man from the *Pictorial* in appropriate rustic terms.

Back in London, St John Cooper consulted none other than Harry Price, the eminent psychic investigator. It could be a poltergeist, the reporter was told. They usually confined their activities to single houses rather than whole communities but there were instances of the infestation of villages. As to the witch exacting some kind of revenge on the community after all these years, Price was sceptical. More likely there had been some release of power after the removal of the stone, perhaps even the community's own unconscious power, roused by the assault on their own heritage. It might be a witch's stone but at least it was *their* witch's stone the Americans had moved.

The following week, the *Sunday Pictorial* concluded the story. SHE'S OUT OF BUSINESS ran the headline. Not much in the way of psychic disturbances had occurred in the last seven days though the witch had had a go at Conrad Moth who found his rabbits

THE WITCH OF SCRAPFAGGOT GREEN 63

roosting along with the chickens in the chicken coop one morning. But that was the end of it. On the night of 11th October, the councillors and assorted villagers went back to the crossroads and manhandled the stone back into place, placing it east and west in the traditional manner, Councillor Sykes, the hard-headed Lancastrian, ensuring the precision of the operation by consulting a compass. There was an additional story, too, that the witch's bones had been discovered and these, it was said, were buried at Little Waltham. And peace, so they tell us, was restored.

But the wicked witch and the dreadful stone have cropped up since.

In 1985 St Anne's Castle Inn was exorcised after several manifestations. The witch was at it, they said. She'd plagued the inn for the past 40 years ever since they had had the stone outside, for after 1944 it had never rested at Scrapfaggot Green in spite of all that had been said. Andy Collins and members of ASSAP (the Association for the Study of Anomalous Phenomena) were called in to the pub. They are alleged to have conjured up the witch and driven her from the building.

In the following year the stone went missing from the pub. The *Essex Chronicle* reminded readers that local lore says that to remove the stone was to release 'the malevolent black witch buried beneath it.' The landlord was mystified. Such a stone could not be moved by fewer than four men, he said. Was this some supernatural force? Some days later the stone was found in the field of a local turkey farmer in Little Leighs.

There is every reason to believe that St Anne's Castle Inn is very heavily haunted. But the witch and her stone seem really to have little to do with it. Many local people who lived in the village before the Second World War had never in their youth and childhood heard of Agnes Haven. Today, these people are highly sceptical of the story put about in the *Sunday Pictorial* in the autumn of 1944.

So what are we to make of this tale of the witch of Scrapfaggot Green? Well, to begin with, over the years there have been accretions to the original account. The haystacks which originally did no more than fall down now appear to have been removed to another field altogether. Now, thirty sheep and two horses were allegedly found dead in a field. Not only did the church clock stop but it went backwards. Cows aborted. Hens stopped laying. Some of these were just the sorts of occurrences for which in the old days innocent women were put to death.

Great Leighs in 1944 – the scene of the Scrapfaggot Green poltergeist disturbances.

But there is a number of queries about the witch and the stone which really need to be cleared up. There certainly was a witch in next-door Boreham. Agnes Haven was tried, at Chelmsford Assizes in July 1593, accused of bewitching John Brett and causing him to be ill. But for using her magic on Edith Hawes, for murdering her by witchcraft, Agnes Haven, really just another victim of ignorance and fear, was hanged. She was not burnt at the stake as some have said. The researches of William Smith, former vicar of Boreham and an extremely careful and conscientious local historian, reveal no instance of witches being burnt at the stake in Essex. Nor is there any evidence to suggest that her execution and burial took place at Scrapfaggot Green. Nor indeed is there any record of the witch's bones being reburied at Little Waltham in 1944.

But perhaps these are mere quibbles. And perhaps doubting the account of the midnight restoration of the witch's stone to Scrapfaggot Green is also a quibble. For if it was replaced there it could not have stayed very long because it very soon found its way to St Anne's Castle Inn where it served as a tourist attraction. Had there been any serious concern about the powers of the stone it is certain that it would never have been allowed to change its venue without some kind of local outcry.

So what about this newspaper tale? Was a reporter making a story out of nothing? Did he encourage gullible country folk to tell him what he wanted to hear? Or was it the other way round? Did the locals string along an innocent Fleet Street man, if such an animal exists? Was there anything in any of this whole sequence of events that could not be explained by rational means? Was it nothing more than the lads of the village – and their fathers – up to mischief?

As for Agnes Haven, the Revd William Smith believes that she was buried without Christian rites, not at Scrapfaggot Green but outside the walls of Boreham church and that bones discovered there during his incumbency were hers. If so, he reburied 'the poor old soul in the churchyard.' And, he says, 'only I know where.'

By the way, if Agnes Haven never was buried at Scrapfaggot Green, then the stone sited there could have had nothing to do with her. Was there ever a witch's stone?

It's all rather dubious. Perhaps now Agnes Haven and her story ought to be allowed to rest.

WHO MURDERED
THE SAILOR?

HOW many are the crimes that are perpetrated with the blessing of governments. So many self-righteous statements are uttered, so many pious defences are mounted. And how well this was demonstrated in the case of the Harwich man, Charles Algernon Fryatt, Master Mariner, captain of several of the ferries belonging to the Great Eastern Railway prior to the First World War and, when the time came, an undoubted hero.

After the outbreak of war in August 1914 the GER merchant ships continued to cross the North Sea to Holland, carrying travellers and some cargo back and forth between the two countries. It is hardly surprising that they were often attacked by enemy submarines. Harwich, a major naval base, was one of the ports from which the precarious trade with the Dutch continued.

The Germans were, however, in something of a dilemma. In the first months of hostilities they did not launch a full-scale attack on British merchant shipping and indeed it was not until 1917 that they were to do so. They did nevertheless harry the GER ferries and other merchant craft. Occasionally there were serious attacks on ships which proved disastrous to the German cause. For instance, the sinking of the British passenger liner *Lusitania* in May 1915 with the loss of 1,200 lives, many of them American, damaged the Germans' reputation permanently in the eyes of many neutrals.

On 3rd March 1915, skippering the SS *Wrexham*, on loan to the GER from the Great Central Railway, Fryatt encountered a U-boat for the first time. The U-boat surfaced and signalled the merchantman to stop. The intention of the U-boat commander was to commandeer the *Wrexham*, using his own men to take the ship into a German-occupied port in Belgium. But Fryatt had other ideas. He ran for it, steaming at 16 knots beyond the reach of the submarine through shoals and minefields, and made his escape. His grateful employers awarded him a gold watch in recognition of his having saved their ship and his exploit was duly recorded in the local press. Fryatt was a local hero.

Within weeks Captain Fryatt was to add to his reputation. This time he was master of the *Brussels*, challenged by U-boat 33 off the Dutch coast. In accordance with international law, the submarine captain had surfaced and signalled to Fryatt and his crew to abandon ship. Should the order be ignored, the German warned, he would fire a torpedo. Fryatt's response was to order the *Brussels* full-ahead, making straight for the U-boat. In haste the German submarine crash-dived, passing under the merchant ship from starboard to port and then immediately resurfacing. It was then so close to its prey that Fryatt was later to say, 'You could easily have hung your hat on the periscope as she lay alongside us.' The U-boat then made off and Fryatt was able to continue about his business.

Whether or not Fryatt struck the German submarine is unclear. Why else did it disappear? Was it damaged? Some of the firemen aboard the SS *Brussels* said that they thought they felt tremors as though the enemy vessel had been struck. The story that went the rounds was that Fryatt had successfully incapacitated the submarine but there is some doubt about this. In fact, it is said the *Brussels* sustained no damage at all.

Whatever the truth of it, Fryatt was once more hailed as a hero in the press. In Parliament, asked a question about the heroics of merchant seamen, Lord Beresford specifically mentioned six merchant skippers, among them Captain Charles Fryatt. Locally, Fryatt was praised as 'The Pirate Dodger'. It was a romantic enough sobriquet, descriptive of the coolness and resourcefulness that people at war expect of their heroes. But it was a nickname that was eventually to rebound on its recipient.

So there was another gold watch and much press coverage of an act that showed that brave Englishmen cared little for the wicked Huns, the barbarians who had shot Nurse Edith Cavell and sunk the innocent *Lusitania*. Not all of the charges levelled in wartime could be justified, of course, but the Germans had executed the nurse and they had needlessly sunk the great ship. But no side ever comes out of warfare as innocently as it enters the fray. Suffice it to say that in addition to the Germans making themselves appear to be wicked, Fryatt and others succeeded in making them appear to be clumsy, cowardly and inept. This was the burden of the propaganda war in British newspapers, just as the German newspapers carried their own versions of whatever had happened. It ought perhaps to be mentioned that the escaping U-boat 33 survived the war, in the course of which it sank 140,000 tons of Allied shipping.

Despite the sustained U-boat war against merchant shipping, contact was maintained between British and Dutch ports. Right until the summer of 1916 Captain Fryatt continued to ply this risky route. Then, on 23rd June 1916, still master of the SS *Brussels*, on his way from the Hook of Holland to Tilbury with a cargo and several refugees, Fryatt was met by five enemy destroyers and torpedo boats. He was in no position to run or to put up any fight. His ship was boarded and taken under escort to the Belgian port of Zeebrugge, then in German hands.

The passengers and crew, including five women stewardesses, were taken to Bruges where they spent two nights in the Town Hall. All but Fryatt were then transferred to Cologne and sent to POW camps. The stewardesses were repatriated after some weeks although the men were imprisoned until the war's end. But Charles Fryatt was detained in Bruges undergoing interrogation while the German military authorities made further enquiries about him. Ah yes, the famous Fryatt, the man who the British authorities had praised for ramming one of their U-boats, they had him now.

At Bruges on 27th July 1916, Fryatt faced a Naval Court under Commander von Yorke. Here, he was charged with attacking U-boat 33. Cited against him were triumphalist cuttings from English newspapers which months earlier had lauded his clever escapes from German submarines. Particularly prominent were references to his ramming the U33 and the awards of watches from the GER's owners and the Admiralty. Captain Fryatt, said the German prosecutor, was not a combatant and therefore had no protection under the terms of the Hague Convention. The proceedings were brief and Fryatt was found guilty as a non-combatant of waging war. The verdict and the death sentence were confirmed at once by the Kaiser. That same evening he was shot by a firing squad.

The Germans were quick to issue the following explanatory notice justifying their action: 'The English Captain of the Mercantile Marine, Charles Fryatt, though he did not belong to

Captain Charles Fryatt, captured by the Germans in 1916.

the armed forces of the enemy, attempted on 28th March, 1915, to destroy a German submarine, running it down. This is the reason why he has been condemned to death by judgment of this day of the War Council of the Marine Corps and has been executed. A perverse action has thus received its punishment, tardy but just. (Signed) Von Schroder, Admiral Commandant of the Corps de Marine, Bruges, 27 July 1916.'

There was outrage in England at the news of Fryatt's execution. In the House the Prime Minister, Asquith, announced his deep regret 'that Captain Fryatt has been murdered by the Germans.' Later he was to announce that his Government would demand 'reparation for this murder.' The word 'murder' was constantly repeated in the press. Lord Claud Hamilton, chairman of GER, spoke in similar terms. 'The latest act of the Hun,' he declared, 'is nothing less than sheer, brutal murder.'

Despite all the accounts that the newspapers had earlier carried, the Government now denied that Fryatt had ever tried to ram the U33. Now there were announcements that the captain 'had saved his vessel and the lives of his passengers and crew by skilfully avoiding an attack, and in recognition of his coolness and judgment the Admiralty made him a presentation.'

In the weeks following the news of the execution, there were frequent references to the murder of Nurse Cavell and the sinking of the *Lusitania*, both of these cited as typical of the barbarous Hun. Fryatt had been shot, so ran the argument, not for sinking a U-boat but simply because he had attempted to do so. But even had he been successful, his supporters went on, he would have been within his rights by the law and custom of the sea. Merchant seamen were allowed to carry armament for self-defence and, as long as they conformed to the rules of war, were accorded the rights of combatants.

The trial was a travesty in the eyes of the Government and the people of Britain. It had been no more than judicial murder. The neutral American Ambassador in Belgium had learnt of the charges against Captain Fryatt and had asked for a postponement of the trial so that a proper defence case with witnesses could be prepared but that was refused. A German officer, a trained lawyer, rather than the representative offered by the Americans, was appointed to defend the Englishman. No witnesses from the U33 could attend the court. Their wartime duties, it was said, meant that they could not be detained ashore.

Yet there are always two sides – possibly more sides – to any argument. Just as the English newspapers expressed their outrage, the German press put their feelings on the matter very strongly. In contrast to *The Times* with its headline 'The Fryatt Murder', the influential *Cologne Gazette* wrote about 'The Punishment of the Pirate Fryatt'.

The German viewpoint was that the U-boat was above water and, in accordance with the international code of naval warfare, had signalled the SS *Brussels* to stop and be searched. In the German version, the *Brussels* allowed the U-boat to approach and then attempted to ram the unsuspecting submarine. It was nothing to do with self-defence but a 'cunning attack by hired assassins'. Throughout their explanations of Fryatt's fate, the Germans were to refer to him as 'a franc tireur, a pirate'. They saw him as equal to a civilian who on land attempts the murder of an enemy soldier and who consequently conflicts with martial law. To protect their submarine fleet the Germans would interpret the law in this way. Honourable and chivalrous combatants, said the German press, needed to be protected against perfidious attacks with the strongest punishment. Fryatt's execution was a necessary and wholesome lesson for Britain.

If the British were convinced that Fryatt was a murder victim then the Germans were equally certain that they had committed no offence. 'The captain who beneath a harmless mask flashes a dagger against an unsuspecting person is a bandit: that he acts on instructions from higher authority does not exonerate him,' was the argument in one newspaper. 'It will probably arouse the same storm of barbarism as was evoked by the Cavell case. That must not disturb us because we have right on our side.' The *Brussels* had never been in danger, the Germans consistently maintained. Fryatt had acted out of vanity and lust for gain, hoping to destroy the German submarine. And were the British themselves not criminals, they asked, when they had on their conscience the recent refusal of a British trawlerman to assist the crew of a sinking Zeppelin?

But what was behind Fryatt's action? He certainly seems to have tried to ram the U33 and it was only after his death that the British Government both denied and tried to justify his action. But the sea war was complex. All British merchant ships had been instructed to paint out their names and port of registry, and when in British waters it was suggested that they fly the flag of a neutral power, preferably the American flag. Furthermore, British vessels were ordered to treat the crews of captured U-boats as 'felons'. They were not to be accorded the status of prisoners of war. In some circumstances, survivors were not to be taken prisoner. They were to be allowed to drown or were to be shot.

Specific orders from the First Sea Lord, Winston Churchill, to Merchant Navy captains, instructed them 'to immediately engage the enemy, either with their armament if they possess it or by ramming if they do not . . . any master who surrenders his ship will be prosecuted.'

Perhaps Charles Fryatt's action is better explained in the light of these orders. Perhaps too the response of the Naval Court in Bruges is better understood. The poor merchant seamen, it seems, had little choice. Fryatt was undoubtedly an English hero. He was at the same time as much a casualty of war as those whose bodies lay in Flanders mud, on the beach at Gallipoli, in African sands.

After the war Captain Fryatt's body was returned from Bruges to Dovercourt where it was buried. He is commemorated by a plaque in Liverpool Street station, yet nowhere is it mentioned that he was as much a victim of his own country's naval policy as that of an enemy nation. Perhaps too it is an irony not solely that the SS *Brussels*, Captain Fryatt's old ship captured by the Germans, was sunk by the British in October 1917 but also that at the end of the war the German U-boat fleet surrendered to Admiral Tyrwhitt at Harwich, the home port of one of that town's most distinguished sailors.

UNSTABLE MATES

O N Saturday, 22nd October 1983, the body of Diane Jones was
found hidden in woodland near Brightwell in Suffolk. A
beater for a pheasant shooting party found her, 35 miles or so
from where she had last been seen three months earlier on 23rd
July.

It took the Suffolk police little time to work out whose body it
was. This was a high-profile disappearance which had taxed their
colleagues across the county boundary. The body found on their
territory was wearing the mauve dress and the high heeled sandals
that Diane had last been seen in. But it took the forensic scientists
rather longer to formally and finally declare that there was no
doubt about the woman's identity. For her face had been so
terribly battered by what the experts decided was a hammer that
she was unrecognisable. Whoever spirited Diane Jones away from
Coggeshall must, in her last minutes, have deeply hated her. The
blows showered on her poor face and head were not simply
intended to kill: they were evidence of a detestation of the
defenceless woman. Was this done by someone who knew her? Or
was it some stranger who picked her up late on that summer's
evening? The case has become a *cause célèbre*. It is still
unresolved. And the two principals, Diane and her husband,
Robert, have been a source of constant interest ever since.

But then, even in Diane's lifetime she was a source of constant
interest. Certainly she was of interest to many men for she was
extraordinarily attractive, a lively intelligent blonde, with a
stunning figure. But she was flawed and one cannot help thinking
that it was the faults in her personality which were to contribute
to her awful death.

Diane had been brought up in Lincolnshire, in beautiful Tealby.
When she first arrived in Coggeshall she must surely have
recognised it as the kind of place she had been raised in.

Coggeshall, where the old wool merchants and the clergy, the farmers and the silk weavers, have left their stamp, should have seemed like a home-coming to her. Its gentle river, its old church, its surrounding countryside had so much in common with Tealby. But Coggeshall has super-eminent charms with its uneven red-tiled roofs; its welter of the most beautifully modest houses with their walls of ochre and blue, of red and saffron; its great barn; its Clock Tower and its many other small delights. What a gem of a place to settle in.

Certainly Diane settled down well with her partner, Paul Barnes, when they arrived in 1978. She commuted daily from their bungalow to Braintree where she was a social worker. Diane, solver of people's problems: how deeply sad that she was ultimately capable only of creating difficulties for herself and for those nearest to her.

Diane had met Barnes, manager of a Chelmsford swimming pool, in 1977 and left her husband, a farm manager, within months. She was to live with Barnes for five years. At some point, she began to drink heavily. As a consequence there were rows, constant show-downs, not just about how she was ruining their lives but how her behaviour was becoming increasingly out of control. And in places like Coggeshall – only 4,000 inhabitants, after all – people talk. Furthermore, it was costly. Barnes was not highly paid. And what if Diane's heavy drinking began to affect her work? What if she lost her job? What then?

Drink was not the sole cause of friction. Diane wanted a baby. She was desperate for a child. But Paul Barnes, who loved her to distraction, was nevertheless all too aware of Diane's imperfections. He believed that she would never be a suitable mother. Increasingly insecure and unstable, she would be a disaster with a child. And then there was depression, blood pressure problems, hysterics, an alleged attempted suicide. Diane must see a doctor. She could not go on in this fashion. So, some time in 1979, she went to see Dr Jones.

Not that she had much faith in Robert Jones. She would sometimes say to Barnes, 'That bloody little fool doesn't understand me.' But perhaps the doctor did understand her. Perhaps what Dr Jones prescribed was not much to her liking. For he was trying to get her to adopt strategies which would take her off alcohol. Not at all to Diane's taste.

But if Diane was not impressed by her 41 year old doctor, he was certainly smitten with her. He was soon to overcome her resistance. After all he lived at elegant Lee's Farm, not in an ordinary little bungalow. And he could afford to take her for extravagant meals. He could introduce her to a different life, a new world.

And Paul Barnes? He had to put up with the love of his life being squired by the doctor. No matter how much he begged and pleaded, he was unable to persuade Diane to remain faithful to him. Nor was Robert Jones's second wife, Susan, able to persuade her husband that he should stand by her. Even arguments that people in the locality would frown at such goings-on had no effect. Robert Jones was totally captivated by his patient. Later he was to claim that he hoped that he was getting her on the right lines, curing her of her addiction, her depression, her high blood pressure. But it was a forlorn hope. As Jones was to say, the idea of ever helping her was 'a romantic notion on my part which just didn't turn out to be true.'

For months Paul Barnes struggled with his errant partner and at one point he went off on his own, leaving her alone at Coggeshall. A brief separation, he must have believed, might bring her to her senses. It seemed not to have done so. In turn, Diane was to ask for time away. She needed time to think over their relationship. When she returned three weeks later, she revealed that she had been to the south of France with Jones.

Now began a curious yo-yo arrangement, with Diane staying sometimes with Paul Barnes and at other times joining Jones at a second house he had bought at Marks Tey. Susan Jones and the two children of their eleven year marriage remained at Lee's Farm, the fine old property on the outskirts of Coggeshall. The wretched Paul constantly wrote to Diane, begging her to break with the doctor. But here was a new life for Diane. There were no anxieties about money. Going out, gadding about, dining expensively, this was a different world. How could a swimming pool manager match it? In September 1980, Diane left Paul for good.

But then a familiar pattern began to emerge. The improvements in Diane's drinking habits that Dr Jones thought that he had succeeded in bringing about, were illusory. He would come home from the surgery to find her drunk, incapable, the house in turmoil. And with the resumed drinking came the familiar abusive behaviour and the rowing over her wanting a child. The arguments that Paul Barnes had been so frequently involved in were being repeated now with Jones. And the doctor was using the same reasons for Diane's not having a child as Paul Barnes had used. She was too unstable for motherhood. Sometimes in the course of their rows she would storm out of the house and return after some days, doubtless with promises to reform. Sometimes she accused him of hitting her. She would show her bruises to friends.

The occasion when one evening Diane, crying, muddied, bruised, called on Barnes was to have curious consequences for the relationship between the two men. Paul went round to see his rival, the man who had dared to strike the woman he adored. He punched the doctor, whose response was not quite what the swimming pool manager had expected. Instead of fighting back, Jones remained calm and called the police. For both men there was some unpleasant local publicity but the result nevertheless was surprising. They discussed the matter and Jones was able to persuade Barnes that he had not been given an exact account of what had happened with Diane. She had fallen off her bicycle, the doctor said. As Jones spoke, Barnes recognised the kind of scene in which the doctor had been involved. He knew it too well, the drinking, the irrational arguments, the shouting and screaming, the pushing, the threats. It was a scenario in which Barnes had all too frequently been involved. But could the two men, the two rivals, not together try to help the woman both of them adored? From then on they met simply to compare notes on her progress, supporting each other in their desperate love for a woman who brought both of them so much unhappiness.

After about six months Susan Jones moved away from Lee's Farm and Jones and Diane moved into the beautiful whitewashed 16th century house. But Diane's behaviour continued to be erratic. And by now, the daily bottles of red wine that had once comforted Diane had been replaced by daily bottles of vodka.

And then, remarkably, Diane was pregnant. Despite all of Jones's determination, it seems that he must have acceded to her request. At Christmas 1981 Diane gave birth to a girl. And she was ecstatic. Was there ever such a wonderful child, such a lovely little girl? Diane, proud and happy, had what she had wanted. All the rows, all the scenes, the unhappiness, all could have been avoided if she could have had this beautiful baby earlier. How proud she was to send photographs of the child to her friends and relatives. What pleasure she had in nursing the babe, in showing her off to the neighbours. And Jones perhaps thought that at last, in spite all of his misgivings, life with Diane would now settle down. For the sake of the baby it must do.

Paul Barnes was called one night to go out for a celebratory drink with Jones. Perhaps he too consoled himself with the idea that from now on Diane would find some real happiness in her life. He had not long been back at the bungalow from having that drink when there was a phone call. It was Robert Jones. Could Paul come up to Lee's Farm at once? There was a bit of a problem with Diane, Jones told him. It was really difficult. Could Paul come over to help?

When Barnes arrived at the farmhouse Jones was desperate. There were some social workers there, called by Diane. In Jones's absence, alone with the baby, she had been unable to cope. She had panicked. She did not know what to do with the baby. All that Diane, that qualified and experienced social worker, could think of doing was to call up her former colleagues.

And that was the end of Diane as mother. Within days a case conference was called by social workers. Diane was declared an unfit mother and her baby was taken into care. She told Paul Barnes that now life had no more value for her.

The rackety, uneven relationship between Jones and Diane rattled on through the succeeding months. For a month in 1982 Diane left Lee's Farm, taking lodgings in Tolleshunt Major. Was this the end of what many now regarded as a hopeless cause? Why did either of them want to prolong the agony? The only possible answer can be that in their haphazard fashion these two loved each other. And the proof of that is that shortly after her return to the farm, they married. As if marriage was to resolve their problems.

Now there was a drink-driving charge. Diane had driven the wrong way down the dual carriageway. Bad enough, but her solicitor was to claim that the fault was not entirely hers. Her marriage to Jones, he alleged, put her under severe emotional strain.

In the winter Diane contacted the *News of the World*. She had a story to tell, protesting in tears that her husband was beating her black and blue, that he no longer wanted her, that on a previous occasion the police had almost charged him for treating her violently.

What a position to place her husband in. When he had first

arrived in Coggeshall, Jones might have been expected to fit in well in such a respectable spot. But he was not everyone's idea of the country doctor. For some he was far too keen on entertaining and high living. Fast living, some might have called it. And his marital arrangements did not meet with everyone's approval. Certainly not in a place like that. His receptionist Susan had been his second wife and then Diane came along and what happened then was regarded as not simply scandalous but outrageous. It was not what Coggeshall expected of its medical men. Where would it all end, people asked.

Where indeed, with Diane increasingly out of control. Her behaviour was shocking by any standards for she now developed the habit of flagging down motorists and when they stopped she invited them to make love to her. This was sheer random flagging down, sheer random sex. She had no idea – from one car to the next – whom she was to couple with. Couple with? As good a term as any for the insatiable, loveless activities she engaged in, in the back of cars, behind hedges, in copses, in fields just off the road. And there were equally random meetings with navvies and Hell's Angels too, all to satisfy her now unquenchable desires. And for those who could provide her with vodka, there were further rewards. Police were later to identify at least 20 of these casual partners but there were others, motorists just passing through, and even local men who it seems never came to the notice of the law.

By the summer of 1983 the marriage was clearly over. A holiday in France seems to have been a last desperate attempt to resolve matters. Diane was two months pregnant and fearful already that her second child would be taken into care. She was well aware of her inability to control the direction of her roller-coaster life. But Jones, confident that she was pregnant with his child, was still hopeful that matters could improve. On their return from holiday, however, nothing had changed and Diane informed her husband that she intended to seek a divorce.

Jones arranged that they would have an intimate meal at home, Lee's Farm, on Saturday, 23rd July. Perhaps he was still hoping to win her back, persuade her to make a fresh start. In preparation Diane, who seemed to be equally excited at the prospect, paid a rare visit to the local hairdressing salon. Normally she did her own hair as prior to qualifying as a social worker she had run her own hairdressing business. The hairdresser was to report Mrs

Jones as being 'either drunk or very weird.' Several regular clients were astonished at her behaviour. Some were amazed when the local doctor arrived to pick her up. Was that his wife? Was that the outrageous Mrs Jones?

The intimate dinner was a disaster. Jones might have foretold it. Diane was so drunk that they were unable to have a sensible discussion about their future. She complained that he never took her anywhere in Coggeshall. Small wonder, for the embarrassments she caused were bad enough beyond the confines of the town. But this evening after the meal, Jones acquiesced when she demanded to be taken to one of the local pubs.

What occurred at the Woolpack comes as no surprise. In that beautiful old oak-beamed bar, only a mile or so from their home, Diane and Jones had a public argument in the course of which Diane is alleged to have fallen off her bar stool into the laps of other customers. Later, when she showed a marked reluctance to go home, Jones picked up their poodle and took it out to the car. When he returned he picked up his wife, threw her over his shoulder and carried her out to the car park.

There are some variations in the account of what happened in the Woolpack. Jones has maintained that Diane was drunk on arriving and even more drunk when he finally took her out. And she was, he has said, foul-mouthed and abusive as she made her exit. Others, however, have denied that she was drunk.

Drunk or no, what now matters is what happened in the few minutes after leaving the Woolpack. Jones has talked about how Diane continued arguing with him on the short journey home. She insisted that she had left her handbag in the pub and demanded to be taken back to retrieve it. Why Jones did not simply drive back to recover the handbag – if it had been forgotten – is wholly understandable. He could hardly go back into the bar where doubtless the absurd and humiliating events were still being talked over, laughed over most likely. How could he walk in there and try to find the handbag with everyone watching?

Somewhere along the drive to the house he pulled up. His account is that Diane got out, saying that she was going back to the Woolpack. She was sick of him, she said, and sick of Coggeshall. He took the poodle for its last walk and returned after six minutes or so to the house expecting to find Diane there.

According to Jones, the house was silent when he returned. He had expected a continuation of their quarrel, Diane at the bottle.

Diane Jones, just a month before she disappeared. (The Times)

But no, there was no sign of her though he searched the house thoroughly. Could she really have gone back to Coggeshall? Would she really have walked back to the Woolpack in her high heeled sandals, in her long flowing summer dress? At that time of night? Was it conceivable? Jones has stuck by the story that it was absolutely conceivable, that Diane's behaviour was predictably unpredictable.

After she left him in the drive of Lee's Farm, Jones never saw Diane again. That is his story and he has through the years stuck by it.

But why did he wait nine days, until 31st July, before reporting to the police that she was missing? The police found that most odd. Not in this marriage, Jones tried to explain. She had left him before now, he said. He imagined that she had gone to stay with a friend and he had been simply waiting for her to turn up again. He had not thought it a matter for the police. After all, he understood that she was due to see her solicitor on the Monday about the divorce. But, said the detectives, Diane had already seen her solicitor on the day before her disappearance. Jones claimed not to know that.

From the outset, the police made it clear that they thought that Jones had somehow done away with his wife. And early on, the press had sniffed out the possibility of a story and had come down to Coggeshall in force.

On 1st August police officers arrived at the red brick bungalow Jones used as the surgery. Even though this was not yet a murder case, they also searched the Peugeot thinking that Diane's body might be in the boot. It was a futile search. Jones had already sold the car. Suspicious? Well, it had been advertised before Diane's disappearance and sold only in the last week. The police succeeded in tracing the new owner of the car. But he had just had it steam-cleaned. Any possible forensic clues were destroyed.

The police search continued, however, at Lee's Farm. The house was thoroughly searched. Even the floor boards were torn up and the chimneys inspected. The garden was dug up: it was over the ensuing weeks to be dug up seven times. A video camera lowered down the well revealed no sign of a body and neither did the mechanical diggers working on the verges of the by-pass. Dogs searched the woods and fields; frogmen searched the reservoir. There were house-to-house enquiries. It was a phenomenally costly search for the body of a woman who no one could at that stage be certain was dead.

Of course there was gossip. Hadn't Diane herself predicted her own death? Hadn't she said that one day she would be killed and the killer would cunningly dispose of her body so that it would never be found? Or had she arranged her own disappearance, just to create a stir? And there were friends in whom Diane had confided. One of them kept notes of her injuries, even a lock of hair allegedly torn out in a fight with her husband. This witness said, though not in court, 'Diane was frightened. There's no doubt about that. She told me he would kill her one day.'

The police were confident that they knew the murderer of Diane Jones. Their pressure and that of the media resulted in Jones saying on television that he had been tempted to confess to the crime. After all, it had been suggested to him that if he pleaded guilty he would not serve long in prison. But he was innocent. Why should he confess to a crime he had not committed?

Oddly enough, the unlikely friendship that Robert Jones and Paul Barnes had established was not damaged either by Diane's disappearance or by her murder. Barnes held to the view that the doctor was innocent of any wrongdoing in this matter. Jones still said that he was confident that Diane would turn up again. The two men continued to meet in pubs as they had done for the past couple of years. The police went on shadowing Jones, certain that he would ultimately make a slip that would lead them to the evidence that would establish his guilt. All they succeeded in doing was to arrest him on a drink-driving charge.

Then on 22nd October, Diane's body was found at Brightwell. Within days Robert Jones was arrested. And so was Paul Barnes, the police unable to understand how it was that the two former rivals could be so friendly. Surely, they thought, Barnes must have picked up some information crucial to their enquiries in all the time he had spent with Jones. Even Susan, Jones's former wife who had remained loyal to him, was taken in for questioning. But all three, after lengthy interviews, were released. Jones, who was questioned for 55 hours, was released on bail.

The murder of Diane Jones has not been solved. In 1984, the Director of Public Prosecutions considered the police files and concluded that there was insufficient evidence to proceed to trial. No murder weapon, no DNA traces have since come to light. The platinum necklace and the gold Omega watch that Diane wore on the night of her disappearance have not been found. Her handbag is still missing.

Robert Jones's life has continued its erratic way, the press always ready to highlight any of his activities. So the public in 1985 was regaled with the story of his latest lover leaving the house to phone the police while he ran off with their nine month old baby. Then there was the momentary stir of anticipation when a new witness came forward with fresh evidence about Diane's murder but after further questioning Jones was released and the story melted away. Readers also shared in the accounts of his fourth marriage. They learnt in 1993 of the latest tragedy in his life when he was struck off the medical register for failing to examine a patient properly. At the time his marriage was crumbling, he was almost bankrupt and, with no professional future, Jones, now a father of five, was being forced to put his house on the market.

There is a sadness about this whole sorry tale of the waste of human potential. There must be blame to be apportioned but in what proportions it is difficult to suggest. But undeniably Diane Jones had the capacity to make a success of her life and so had Robert Jones. That they both failed so comprehensively is a matter of profound regret.

As to who killed Diane Jones, that remains a mystery.

POLTERGEISTS

A T least with that old Roman centurion who comes marching across the causeway that links the mainland with Mersea you have some idea of who he is – or was – and you can even vaguely accept that you are seeing him because some trick of time and place affects both you and him. He wouldn't, in other words, be there unless you and your brain and nervous system were ready at that precise moment to receive him. Or look at it this way, for some curious reason he keeps reprising the same old moment down the years. There's no future for him and no past. It is as if a few inches of an old film reel were being played over and over again.

There are scores of ghosts. There's a huge cast of nuns and monks, robbers and ladies in grey; there are winsome milkmaids and chaps in tights; as well as more up-to-date apparitions. Some of course are those dead who are stranded here, unaware of their situation; others play out the few seconds or minutes of some past real-life drama where they underwent some or other agony of spirit or body. But in the main there is much to be said for the idea that apparitions are the consequence of some kind of confusion, coincidence, conjunction perhaps, between a place and the past and present.

Well, these are ways of looking at ghosts and perhaps regarded like that they need not worry those who come across them. But poltergeists are different. They don't have the loyal attachment to places that apparitions appear to have. Nor is their presence so easily understood. Their activity is inexplicable, infuriating and the effect on those they visit is often profound. At least with an apparition there is some chance of understanding that its appearance is located in some moment of the past. In the course of robbery, Dick Turpin tortured an old lady at Trap's Hill Farm at Loughton, and ever since his ghost and that of his victim are said to appear riding furiously down the hill on his horse. So, there's an historical event which has some basis in fact and it may be that the terror of the moment has engraved itself on the place. Or there is the ghost of a girl killed in a car at Kent Elms Corner at Southend whose apparition has given rise to several phantom hitchhiker tales. But again, the apparition comes out of some true event. Then there was the ghost of the fire chief at Greys who was so attached to his former workplace that he appeared there from time to time, years after his death, in officer's uniform. Again, a link with a real past.

Poltergeists do not seem to have this link with any recognisable happenings in the past. It is therefore difficult to understand their purpose when they arrive. But they do make their presence known.

At Langenhoe church, referred to earlier in this book, the Revd Ernest Merryweather had many experiences of a supernatural nature. For example, he saw the apparition of a woman on a number of occasions. But he also experienced many poltergeist manifestations. One day in the church he saw his penknife, lying on the ground in front of him. Immediately before, it had been in his pocket. Like many poltergeist tricks – and this word 'tricks' is not an inappropriate word to use – this seems pointless. Poltergeist performances are rather like the irritating antics of a small boy trying to show off some little skill he has mastered. Because the things that poltergeists get up to so often seem to be petty. Why, if they are so clever, don't they confine themselves to things on a larger scale?

Still, one has to admit there is something pretty classy in the supernatural line if a penknife can be made to pass through the material of a man's jacket. Matter has been made to pass through matter, a 'trick' verified on many occasions by those investigating poltergeists. But capable of the classy or no, the antics of poltergeists very frequently have something of the immature about them. Instead of something on the grand scale, they resort instead, for example, to stone throwing. There were regularly showers of stones being flung about the place at Borley. And bottles too. Or take the house in Abbots Road in Colchester where the parcels were removed from under the Christmas tree and put in another room. And in the same house, an air freshener flew from the downstairs lavatory across a passage and into the kitchen before falling gently to the floor. This is, in a way, quite impressive

Poltergeist activity in the news.

because the freshener was required to negotiate bends and corners but it does have the smack of the prank about it as if the perpetrator were saying 'Hey, look at me! Aren't I clever?' It's small stuff, isn't it?

At times it appears that a company of low-grade magicians have decided to go through their rather shallow routines. Lights go off and on; sounds of falling cutlery and china are heard yet on investigation there is no evidence of any disturbance; clocks and ornaments on mantlepieces are turned to face the wall; a film cassette suddenly leaves its resting place on a window sill and flies across the room. All of these have been recorded in the most ordinary of homes. At the much haunted Three Chimneys in Clacton, many years ago, all of the chairs, placed at night under the tables, were found next day to have been placed on the table tops. There does not appear to be any great intelligence at work here, does there? And what about the house at Stansted Mountfitchet where in the 1940s the young children were taken out of their beds and placed under the table? But despite the fact that their tricks are quite low-level, poltergeists are genuinely frightening. Their presence throws households into the deepest despair and anxiety. It is the randomness of their activities and their frequent defiance of the very laws of nature that drives people from their homes.

In Cliff Town Road in Southend, Mrs Kathleen Orchard found that flowers had been taken from their vase in the night and laid out in a line, stripped of their leaves. 'I was in bed when I heard a noise. I just thought it was the dog shuffling. But in the morning I found the flowers.' In the church at Langenhoe flowers being got ready for the altar were similarly moved surreptitiously. And it is strange that on frequent occasions these movements of objects are completed without anyone seeing them being disturbed.

There are instances too of levitation. John and Sue Day of Aveley (see The Aveley Encounter in this book) were amazed one night to see their television set rise in the air though they were probably less surprised than the Clacton woman who lived in Burrs Road. She was sitting in a rocking chair, nursing a baby, when suddenly the chair began to lift off. Her head nearly touched the ceiling. Nevertheless, she jumped down and ran to the door but could not open it. Some force prevented her. Another not untypical example of poltergeist-work. And there are many instances – not least at Borley Rectory – where doors have been found unaccountably locked or where some apparent force will not permit unlocked doors to open.

Walter and Edna Johnson and their two teenage children Doreen and Jonathan were forced out of their Havering home in 1972. Plates were thrown across the room; sugar bowls were emptied on the floor; objects fell from shelves; the bedclothes were pulled off them in the middle of the night and on one occasion Doreen was flung out of bed by some force.

Several years ago another Johnson family who lived in Abbotts Drive in Stanford-le-Hope were pestered by a poltergeist. Knives, scissors and a hammer disappeared at different times only to turn up again in some unexpected part of the house. Once, Oxo cubes disappeared from a kitchen cupboard and then just as mysteriously reappeared. In some areas of the house there were icy cold spots. There were three teenage children in the family and many of those who have studied poltergeist phenomena have attributed them to adolescent tensions, the anger, frustration and aggression felt by many youngsters reaching puberty. There being no opportunity for the adequate release for such powerful emotions, they are vented unconsciously as a kind of random energy. Thus, some would say that one of the younger Johnsons, quite unbeknown to himself, was the source of the odd occurrences in his home.

The theory that the activity of poltergeists emanates from adolescent angst needs some qualifying. Perhaps young people are more frustrated generally than are adults. But there is good evidence that the presence of adolescents is not essential for such phenomena. Adults too have been at the centre of poltergeist manifestations. Adults may in general handle their tensions rather better than young people but not all do. The argument that the emergence of poltergeists depends on the human temperament and its ability to handle frustration seems persuasive.

Or are there certain intelligences, probably non-human, which feed off the uncertain emotional lives of men and women? Or from the innate psychic capacities of certain people?

Remember Ernest Merryweather who was rector of Langenhoe? He had several experiences of poltergeist activity when alone in the church – missing objects, unaccountable crashing sounds and the like. Yet he does not seem to have been a man with an especially tortured emotional life. So how was it that he attracted such manifestations? Might it be that he possessed some powerful psychic gifts? Certainly several young people who have been the centre of poltergeist activity have in later life developed significant mediumistic powers.

At least, there is some small comfort for those who are visited by poltergeists. They tend not to stay for long. Do they simply fade away as people's frustrations usually do? If they are emotional in essence they may simply yield to the passing of time. Deep jealousies, rages, fears, in most cases all pass away for what do we become if they do not? Do the poltergeists pass away with them? Do they then go away? Or do they, unlike ghosts which in some cases hang around for centuries, take off for some other venue, some other temporarily receptive vessel?

When natural laws are turned upside down and when we are incapable of explaining why this should be so, we are left feeling so helpless.

THE DISAPPEARANCE OF
CONSTANCE KENT

IT was dangerous, no doubt about that. Church Cottage was in so dilapidated a condition that there were very real fears that one day it would fall down and somebody, a child from the school most likely, would be injured or killed. It would have to come down. Even back in 1928 when the present owner had moved in it had caused the local surveyor grave misgivings.

Easy enough for the local authority to order its demolition, save that the owner would have to be notified. And where was the owner? Nobody could say. No-one had seen her for ten years. In 1939 – in the spring of that year, some thought – she had just disappeared from Fingringhoe, that scattered, thinly populated village, south of the Colne estuary. And after one or two half-hearted attempts to trace her, she had been completely forgotten.

Poor Constance Kent. Not that anyone cared very much. Old, unkempt, reclusive eccentrics do not really rouse great anxieties when one day they appear to have been spirited away off the face of the earth. And anyway, she was not the kind of woman to tell anyone her plans. If Constance Kent had suddenly made up her mind to leave her three-roomed cottage she had lived in since 1928, she would not have bothered to inform anyone.

But in 1949 there was a serious attempt to get in touch with her. The demolition order could not be carried into effect until she had been made aware of it. The matter now seemed pressing to the local authority. After all, Church Cottage which was on the roadside was sited on a plot of land used by the nearby school's pupils as a playground. And it was well enough known locally that, despite all of the headteacher's injunctions, boys and girls went inside to play from time to time. Some day, the adults warned, someone was going to be seriously hurt.

But after all these years Constance Kent eluded all who sought

The overgrown and neglected cottage in Fingringhoe where Constance Kent once lived.

her. Was she alive or dead? Would she be found at a friend's house? From time to time she had been known to visit friends though she had never indicated where these might live. Was she resting in some distant graveyard? Or would her remains be found in some copse or creek, in a ditch or a shed? Such speculation, but no Constance Kent. The matter was becoming desperate. The police were called in.

It was Detective Superintendent Totterdell and Detective Inspector Kemp who decided to make a thorough inspection of the now notorious little two-storey building in which Constance Kent had lived. On the day of their arrival at the cottage, however, the word was out. The press had already set up their headquarters in the Whalebone, the pub opposite. There was a big story here, they were sure. And as Totterdell and his assistant entered the tiny cottage, the press men followed them. But Totterdell was a wise old bird. The two policemen stayed for only a short time before going back to their station. Then, in the early hours, they returned to make a methodical inspection of the premises, unencumbered by the attentions of Fleet Street.

The detectives found the passageway littered with the remains of years-old correspondence. Little of it could be read, however. The rats and mice which now infested the house had taken care of that. On the table in one of the downstairs rooms there was a plate. On it was a ten year old meal, hard, discoloured, indistinguishable as food, and still not entirely devoured by the rodents, the flies, the insects. The dust hung heavy over every surface; the cloying smells of the years, the damp, the rot, the decay, were palpable.

Upstairs was the narrow bedroom, 14 feet by 6 feet 3 inches. There was a single bed down one wall. The blankets still lay there under plaster fallen from the ceiling. It was clear that it had not been slept in for the blankets had not been turned back. Along the opposite wall were a wash-stand, a chair piled with newspapers and a dressing table. Here the plaster from the ceiling was everywhere. And in the narrow space between the bed and the wash-stand, almost hidden under debris, there was a skeleton and what appeared to be clothing. Constance Kent?

The skull was cemented to the floor by fragments of mummified flesh to which were attached strands of dark hair. Some of the bones had been eaten by rats; others were intact. The right arm, still covered by skin and dried muscle, was slightly raised as though in some kind of salute. The trunk was covered in rotted clothing. Some of the clothing – underclothes, it turned out – still retained the safety pins which their owner had used to keep them in place.

But could this be Constance Kent? Could she have remained there in that narrow gangway between bed and wash-stand for ten years? There had been people enough in the cottage time and again, one or two genuinely seeking the old woman; there had been a neighbour and two policemen; and what must have added up to dozens of children. What about some of the servicemen who had been stationed nearby and who from time to time had used the empty building for soldierly dalliances. Had none of these people ever seen the remains? Had no one even suspected that the old woman might be there?

After the preliminary inspection the human remains were sent off to the Department of Anatomy at the London Hospital Medical School where they were examined and later reported on at the inquest by Dr Francis Camps, the Home Office pathologist and his associate, Dr H. E. Holden. The garments were sent to the Metropolitan Police Forensic Science Laboratory.

Meanwhile, back in Essex, Totterdell and Kemp continued their enquiries. They had to be certain that these were Constance Kent's remains that they had uncovered. So who was Constance Kent? Why had she not been found earlier?

There were some who still remembered the missing woman. She was a local woman, it transpired, born in the village in 1871. That was no real surprise. But it might have surprised some to learn that the odd and uncommunicative old creature, who for much of her time cut herself off from the outside world, had once been an actress, with the stage name, Vera Verscayle. Not an outstandingly prominent actress, it must be admitted, but at least someone capable of standing on stage and communicating with strangers in the darkness beyond the footlights. Communicating? Constance Kent?

Most who now recalled her had known her as a sallow-faced woman with long black hair and prominent teeth, a deaf old soul who, on those rare occasions when she was obliged to speak to others in the village, used an ear trumpet. Oh yes, they could remember her still, remember her stooping walk, the way she dragged her feet. They could recall the air of quite deliberate self-neglect, the old felt hat, the dark, ankle length dress. And they recalled how nearly every day she called in at the Whalebone for a packet of Woodbines. It was perhaps her only regular contact with anyone in Fingringhoe.

The headmistress at the school from 1921 until 1940 was Miss Ethel Donnan and she was sought out by the detectives in 1949. She remembered Constance Kent well enough. And she remembered clearly how the children had come to her one day after the old woman's disappearance to complain about the 'stink' from the cottage. She had wondered at the time if it wasn't rats and had reported the matter. A sanitary inspector sent to investigate in January 1940 had found no signs of rats but it may be that he did not explore the upstairs of the cottage.

On other occasions, Miss Donnan told the detectives, some of the girls had been distressed. The boys had been telling them that they should not go into the cottage because Miss Kent was lying in there, dead under the bed. They had seen her hair. The headteacher had told the girls not to be so silly. The boys were just trying to frighten them, she had told them, but they ought not of course to go into such a run-down building.

A couple of former pupils, Derek Allen and Ian Hopkins, had

been eleven year olds in 1939. They told the detectives that in the autumn of that year they had often gone into the cottage when playing hide-and-seek. They had entered either through the back door or through a broken window. Hopkins recalled the bedroom with its wardrobe and dressing table. Under the bed he had seen a pile of what had looked like rags or old clothes. He had heard talk of a skeleton in the cottage though he had not seen any signs of one. Derek Allen was sure that he had seen bones under the bed but had never suspected that they might be human. But would Constance Kent, if it was her, have been reduced to a skeleton in a few short months? Unlikely. Then how was it that the boys did not see a recognisable corpse between the bed and the washbasin? It's a mystery.

But what a place for boys to play in. Think of the thrill of it, the scariness of it, being up there in that empty cottage alone, hiding, half-hoping to be caught and released from this place about which there were such tales. Tales of a woman's hair, of a skeleton, of a corpse under the bed . . . wait till they told those girls.

But others had called in at the cottage with a more serious purpose. Some time in the early summer of 1939 the wife of the licensee at the Whalebone told Mrs Maskell, a friend of Constance Kent, that she had not seen the old woman for several weeks. Mrs Maskell, who had come over from Colchester specifically to find out why she had not seen her friend for such a time, went to Church Cottage but could not get in. There was no trace of anyone but knowing her friend to be a very private person she was not especially worried at that point. In August Mrs Maskell visited the cottage once more and managed to enter by the back door but again there was no sign of Constance Kent and no indication of where she might be.

Some months later, in the early days of the war, Reuben Wyncoll, who lived nearby, told the local constable that the cottage had been broken into, that children had been inside on several occasions and had done considerable damage. The policeman accompanied Wyncoll to Church Cottage and together they inspected the building. They had found the back door insecure – small wonder if boys were in and out playing hide-and-seek – and the downstairs window broken. The front door they found to be locked but with the key inside. One of the downstairs rooms was in disorder and the living room untidy. Papers on the tables, chairs and floors had been chewed by rats. Upstairs they found the bedroom fairly tidy. On the dressing table Wyncoll noticed a pension book to which, he was later to claim, he drew the policeman's attention. The roof was intact and there was no smell. Evidently at that point the ceiling had not fallen in.

And they did not see anything? Well, the constable was later to say that they had not been looking for a body. Nor had the boys seen a body.

Several years later Reuben Wyncoll accompanied by another police officer inspected the cottage again. The children were still breaking in and causing damage, he said. The roof at that time was still intact and apart from the damp, there was no particular smell. But no body was seen.

And this was about as far as Superintendent Totterdell got in his investigation. At the inquest the jury were satisfied that the remains tallied with the descriptions they had received of Constance Kent. The black hair, the prominent teeth, the indications from the laboratory that the body was that of a deaf woman, somewhat rheumatic, all convinced the jury that they were pronouncing on Constance Kent. The very clothing, those bits and pieces of rotted cloth which had survived the years, also suggested that they had been worn by someone who took no pride in her personal appearance.

And cause of death? Impossible to say. But natural causes, the pathologists had no hesitation in declaring. There was no suspicion of foul play. It was likely, they suggested, that Constance Kent had been resting on the bed, fully dressed, apart from her shoes. Somehow she had fallen out, possibly dislocating her shoulder. Had she perhaps lain for some time unconscious? Had she roused herself, called out for help time and time again? Had she finally succumbed, unable to raise herself from the narrow space into which she had fallen? Perhaps. In any event, an open verdict was returned.

But it is a mystery all the same. How was it that it took ten years to find the old woman's corpse? Those boys, the friend, the neighbour, the policemen . . . and Constance Kent under their very noses for all that time. And the stories that boys were telling the girls all those years before . . . stories of a corpse under the bed, of a skeleton, of a hank of hair that they had seen.

Where did such stories come from?

JACK

*I*T'S *always Jack. It's always him, waiting in the shadows, flitting through our dreams, haunting the nightmare alleys of memory. Jack's the one who set the standard against which all the rest are measured. Always Jack. Always with us.*

Jack? Jack who?

Why Jack the Ripper, of course, that's who.

But first here's William Gull. Let's have a look at him. According to some experts, there was more to this eminently respectable old chap than meets the eye. Some in fact say that he was . . . but, wait, let's have a look at him first.

On 3rd February 1890 they brought Sir William Gull's body up by train from Liverpool Street station so that he could be buried in Thorpe-le-Soken, the small Essex town where he had been born and where other members of his family were buried. Later in the day a special train conveyed members of the aristocracy, government ministers, the elite of the scientific and medical world in which he had achieved such distinction. Wreaths, including one from the Prince and Princess of Wales, decked the simple churchyard where crowds of locals gathered at the last resting place of one of Thorpe's most celebrated sons. And from such humble beginnings, too, for Gull, the youngest of eight children, was born in 1816 on his father's barge, *The Dove*, at the time tied up at St Osyth Mill in the parish of St Leonard, Colchester. So there were no distinct privileges for this Essex lad.

Yet despite such significant lack of advantage, in an age in which birth and connections meant so much, William Gull was to become one of the foremost medical men of his time. He was a Fellow of the Royal Society, a Fellow of the Royal College of Physicians and Professor of Physiology at Guy's. In the course of his long career he attended to many eminent men and women. In 1871, he was responsible for the treatment of the Prince of Wales during a threatening attack of typhus. In consequence of this he became a baronet. Sir William Gull's final distinction was his appointment as Physician-in-Ordinary to Queen Victoria.

An enviable career one must admit. To rise from such beginnings can command nothing but admiration and respect and yet there were rumours, stories, relating to events in his last years which clung to Gull's reputation. Indeed, they attached to Gull up to quite recent times at Thorpe-le-Soken and in the world at large for that matter.

For example, some have said that Gull was never buried on that early February day. Some hinted that another man's body was interred. Others have claimed that nothing but a coffin full of stones went into the ground while Gull himself, under an assumed name, was confined in some private madhouse. Could it be so? Could such a tortuous trick have been played out? But by whom? And why?

Writer Stephen Knight visiting the churchyard in the 1970s spoke to the verger who commented: 'This is a large grave, about twelve feet by nine, too large for two people [Gull and his wife]. Some say more than two are buried here. It is big enough for three, that grave.' He went on to tell Knight: 'Burial places for two aren't normally that big. Of course it's possible that somebody else is buried there without anyone knowing who.'

A third body in the grave? There is no record of anyone but Gull and his wife in that plot.

Other researchers came across a strongly held belief in Thorpe-le-Soken that whoever was buried in February 1890, it was not Sir William Gull. Many believed that it was several years later that he was put into the grave in circumstances of great secrecy.

Mysteries then. Rumours lingering 80, 90 years after the man's supposed burial.

The will, for example. It was, very naturally, probated in 1890 but why, when nothing seems to have changed, was it probated a second time in 1897? Is that when Gull really died? Had he been, as some have suggested, locked away insane all those years?

And another curious fact – Gull's death certificate was signed by his son in law, Dr Theodore Dyke Acland. Whilst not illegal, it was unusual for a relative to sign such a document. After all when Gull died – or when he is alleged to have died – there were other medical men present.

But the real mystery that has attached to Sir William Gull is something more significant than an important figure in the world of medicine being placed in a Victorian insane asylum.

In April 1895 the *Chicago Sunday Times-Herald* ran a story about the mystic, Robert James Lees, who claimed to have taken a detective to a house in London where a distinguished physician had lived. This physician, Lees claimed, had been placed in an insane asylum under the name of Thomas Mason. His death had been announced and a fake funeral held.

And this subterfuge was to cover up the identity and the fate of the serial killer known variously as 'Leather Apron', 'The Whitechapel Murderer' or most famously of all as 'Jack the Ripper'. And some have asserted, and presumably have been asserting since 1895, that Sir William Gull was that man.

There has been great speculation down the years about Jack's identity. Much of the early evidence, taken in times when record keeping was less fastidious, has been lost. Some documents were taken as souvenirs; others were destroyed when the case was closed in 1892 and it was assumed that it would never be resolved. The Blitz took care of other written evidence. Indeed, it is not totally unfair to suggest that much of what we 'know' about the Ripper comes from the researches and speculations of more recent days. But some of these researchers write about material deliberately destroyed or hidden. What was so secret about Jack?

Jack was the first serial killer to catch the public imagination, the first one to be written up in the newspapers, especially *The Times* and the *Daily Telegraph*, with such relish that he came to find a lasting place in our national mythology. Yet it is not really certain how many women he slew. Estimates vary between four and nine but five is the generally accepted figure, all done to death in the tiny area of Whitechapel, Spitalfields, Aldgate and City of London between the late summer and late autumn of 1888. August to November, just a short few weeks to make his name, to become, in fact, one of the immortals.

Forensic evidence indicates that all of the victims were strangled standing, facing a man they took to be a client. They were then lowered to the ground and Jack's work began. He now cut their throats, taking his knife from the right hand side. The extensive and ferocious mutilations to the abdomen of several of the women were also from the right. It seems that by operating in this way, with his victims on the ground, he had less chance of bloodying himself. Does this suggest some awareness of surgery?

Like many serial killers he took trophies too. On one occasion it was a kidney, cut out unusually enough from the front, though without causing damage to any other organs. On another occasion he removed the sexual organs with one bold, confident stroke.

Imagine, only one of his five acknowledged killings was inside a house. The others were in yards, dank alleyways, out in the open, at dead of night.

Jack's surgery was inevitably hurried for fear of being caught. It took place in poor light. Whilst at the time there was some disagreement about his surgical skills, it is generally accepted that here was a man of some considerable skill going about his work.

Gull?

Well, Sir Melville McNaughten, Chief Constable in 1894, never even considered Gull to be a suspect in a confidential report on the unsolved crimes. But then what if the Ripper's identity was known to a select band of people? What if there were considered to be pressing reasons to protect the Ripper? What if even McNaughten was in some kind of plot to conceal the identity of the murderer? This is certainly a highly popular view, this romantic tale of a conspiracy which reached and touched the highest in the land.

Stephen King's *Jack the Ripper: The Final Solution*, published in 1978, propounds this theory. He claims that Joseph Sickert, son of Walter Sickert, the Victorian painter, told him the outline of the story and that having researched it thoroughly he accepted broadly what he had been told. Melvyn Fairclough's gripping *The Ripper and the Royals* which came out in 1991 covers even more of this ground.

The story involved Prince Albert Victor, the Duke of Clarence, who was himself at one time a likely candidate in some researchers' eyes as the Ripper. But the evidence clears the Duke. The involvement of Eddy, as he was familiarly known, was according to Knight and Fairclough nevertheless real. Joseph Sickert explained to them, at different times, that the prince and Sickert's father used regularly to frequent the East End of London. The bisexual prince, acting incognito, enjoyed himself in the shadier parts of town. But then, the story goes, he met Annie Crook, fell in love with her, married her secretly, and there was a baby, Alice Margaret. Naturally this arrangement was kept secret for how could a prince of the realm, son of the heir to the throne, grandson of Victoria, possibly marry a commoner? And a

Sir William Gull, Physician-in-Ordinary to Queen Victoria. An eminent son of Thorpe-le-Soken but was he 'Jack the Ripper'?

Catholic at that.

And when the news ultimately leaked to Queen Victoria she insisted that action be taken. She called on her prime minister, Lord Salisbury.

Action, ma'am, but what action? he might have said.

But, again according to the Sickert/Knight/Fairclough account, that was left to him to decide.

Joseph Sickert told Knight how the house in Cleveland Street where Eddy and Annie and their baby were installed was suddenly raided. Eddy was taken away in one cab, the bewildered Annie in another to begin a tragic and awful downward descent. The baby, little Alice Margaret, was smuggled away to the care of nuns by her nursemaid, Mary Kelly.

The story then swings on to Mary Kelly who herself in turn goes into a downward spiral of drink and prostitution. And maudlin Mary, unable in drink to keep the information to herself, tells her friends all about the Duke and his wife and the baby and the raid. And her friends, tut-tutting, say how dreadful it is and how immoral and shouldn't something be done about it. And they're all on the game but artless enough and they think the government ought to fork out a few quid because it's awful what they've done.

So the great government conspiracy comes into operation again. Having saved Eddy from his worst self, and having silenced Annie by having Gull perform operations on her brain, they are now confronted by these dreadful prostitutes demanding cash.

So Jack is no solitary madman stalking prostitutes. He is an agent of the government, protecting the security of the state and the good name of the royal family. They say that at the head of the conspiracy is Lord Randolph Churchill. But the workman, the butcher, is Gull, that staunch servant of the Crown, who goes out at night to his work, sitting in a coach driven by John Netley who used to take Eddy out on his East End jaunts. And inside the coach with Gull is Eddy's boon companion, Walter Sickert, who will act as look-out whenever one of these treacherous women is being attended to.

They are all of them, these women, common prostitutes, given to drink and for most of their days destitute. They live in common lodging houses or workhouses and from time to time, driven by their inevitable health problems, they are in infirmaries. All of them, save the last victim, are in their mid-forties.

On the last day of August, Mary Ann Nichols meets Jack in a narrow cobbled street and is only, according to the police report, 'slightly mutilated'. Less than a fortnight later 'Dark Annie' Chapman encounters him and is left with some of her entrails round her neck. Catherine Eddowes and 'Long Liz' Stride meet their ends on the same day, 30th September. And 25 year old 'Ginger', Mary Jane Kelly, was the last victim. She lets him into her squalid little room and she most of all suffers the most ghastly mutilation. Remember her? She was the nursemaid of little Alice Margaret. And so now, with the last of the potential blackmailers done to death, Jack is able to retire, Gull to return to respectability. Only a few weeks of the dying year, that's all it takes. In that time the women are despatched and Gull can resume a normal life. Annie, increasingly insane, survives in poverty for the next 30 years.

At least that is a compelling and persuasive version of the famous tale, debunked by many serious Ripperologists but popular with those who enjoy late-flowering Gothic horror laced with conspiracy theory. But there are questions. For instance, there are a few elementary questions to be asked about Sir William Gull.

The first is that if you wished to hire an assassin would you choose a man whose whole life had been eminently respectable? Would you expect him to act in this ultimately depraved manner? Would you think that the ideal man to select for this hazardous task would be 70 years of age? And would you not think, even if he fitted in all other respects, that a man who had recently given up his medical practice after suffering a stroke was entirely unsuited for such work?

Gull's story certainly has some odd features. The will, for example; the size of the grave; the possibility even that he did not die in 1890 but was committed to an asylum – all these seem to be worthy of enquiry. But none of it really adds up to his being more than an eminent medical man. It certainly does not make him a convincing or suitable candidate for the world's best known serial killer.

One of the most distinguished of those who lie in the graveyard at Thorpe-le-Soken really does seem to have been ill-treated by posterity. He does not deserve so ill a reputation. But he does, nevertheless, leave some interesting questions.

ANYTHING CONSIDERED

'LADY, late 30s, seeks part-time employment in or around Maldon. Own transport. Anything considered. Previous experience banking. Able to type. Phone XXXX.'

It certainly was not boredom that led Josephine Backshall to insert the advertisement in the Situations Wanted columns of the *Maldon and Burnham Standard* in early 1974. She already led a full enough life. In addition to running the semi-detached house in Norfolk Close in Maldon she had a clerical job in the town. Furthermore she belonged to the choir at the church that she and the children attended regularly. She was also a member of a Scottish country dancing group and a Brownie leader. In some measure it must have been to find further outlets for her bounding energy and enthusiasm that led this attractive, home-loving woman to place the advertisement. And of course there was the consideration that it would contribute to the family finances for although her husband Mike was in full and regular employment at Ford's, they had three children, Claire aged 7, Paula 10 and John 12 to bring up.

It is difficult to imagine precisely what kind of work Josephine was hoping for. Perhaps some baby-sitting would be on offer. Possibly someone might need some typing, a restaurant want menus or a student a thesis. Or perhaps she might be offered counter-work. Anything really. Not necessarily on a regular basis because that would not be possible, given her existing commitments. It is self-evident that some of the offers she might receive would not be suitable. But she could pick and choose. If anyone bothered to respond.

But almost immediately there was a response and it was more encouraging than Josephine had expected. Some days after the appearance of the advertisement a man rang and talked about the possibility of modelling for cosmetics and possibly clothing. He was called Peter, a photographer, looking for mature models. Would Josephine consider that kind of work?

Now this was different. This was not what she had expected. It was in a different league from baby-sitting; it was not in the same street as copy-typing. This was infinitely more exciting. She could imagine herself appearing in clothing catalogues, modelling dresses or suits, possibly holding exotic bottles of perfume. Undoubtedly excited, she made an appointment to meet Peter the following week at Witham, 15 miles away from her home.

For Josephine Backshall, that energetic, loving mother and wife, the prospect of a whole new world was opening out. With typical enthusiasm she set off for her appointment in Witham.

And no one turned up.

Imagine the disappointment, the nagging sense of humiliation as she drove home, the sense of embarrassment when she told Mike. Surely, she must have thought, the man could have telephoned. If he had decided not to go through with the idea could he not have made some excuse rather than expose her to such a let-down?

And then next day there was a phone call. It was Peter. There was an apology, an explanation. This was not the way in which he normally treated ladies, the caller told Josephine. He couldn't afford to be dismissive of them, not in his line of work. He was in a business directly focused on ladies, he told her; she had to understand, he said, how badly he felt about what had happened . . . and so on. He must have been persuasive, convincing enough for her to agree to another appointment. After all, this was no artless teenage girl but an experienced 39 year old he was talking to. Perhaps a younger girl would have slammed down the phone; perhaps it was because she was so mature Josephine came to understand the difficulties of her potential employer. And there was, of course, another consideration. The money that was on offer was too generous to be thrown away just because of some silly mistake. Yes, she would meet him.

Again he failed to arrive at their rendezvous.

And Mike just shook his head, wondering if the chap could be serious. Was he having her on? Was he just some kind of stupid hoaxer? Who was this man making promises of really good payments that were likely to follow if she was suitable? Why did she not forget the whole business?

But in early March there was yet another call. And once more

Peter poured out his reasons for not turning up and again Josephine seems to have been thoroughly convinced by what he said. Yes, she must have told him, it was all right. Yes, such things happened. Could Josephine come to Witham one evening? He wouldn't let her down this time. Yes, of course she could.

He'd never turn up. That was Mike's view.

But this time he did.

Josephine and Peter had a drink together in Witham. He apologised again for the inconvenience, the disappointment. There was work for her, he promised. He was setting it up. These things took time. In the meantime, to make up for all the trouble she had been put to, he had a little present for her. He handed Josephine a sum of money by way of compensation.

At home Mike continued to express his doubts but Josephine assured him that Peter was a perfectly decent sort of man, quite a good sort really. There was nothing to worry about, she told him.

Josephine also talked to her friends about Peter and her new prospects, mentioned the possibilities of promotions for well-known cosmetics. Later, the police were to find the word 'Palmolive' written on a telephone pad at home. Another promotion? Even more glamorous work?

Josephine also described the man to Mike and to her friends. She most certainly called him Peter though some had the impression that he was called David. What did he look like? He was tall, heavily built, possibly in his mid-thirties, Josephine said. Quite personable.

In the course of the summer Josephine met Peter on at least one other occasion. He telephoned to ask if he could visit her at home for a photographic session. She later mentioned that he had taken photographs in the garden, that they had talked about modelling for catalogues and that he had seemed highly satisfied with her, thought she had promise. There was another photo session at Beeleigh Falls in Maldon which Peter had said reminded him of his childhood. From what she said Peter used an expensive, single-lens, reflex camera. He'd be in touch again, he had told her.

And he was in touch.

On Tuesday, 29th October 1974, he rang. As it was half-term Josephine had come home from work at midday to give the children their lunch. It was then that she received a phone call. One of the children heard her say, 'Peter, what are you doing in Coggeshall?' A later police check suggested that the mysterious

Josephine Backshall.

Peter had rung from the Old Swan pub at Bradwell, near Coggeshall.
Could she meet him that evening? He was sorry about the short notice. Some difficulty, it seems. He'd been let down by a woman who had been going to do some modelling for him in Cheltenham that night. Could she help? There was talk of £100 commission. This was more than pin-money and even if it was not top-drawer modelling, it promised to be more glamourous than anything Josephine had previously experienced. She must have thought that at last, after several months of waiting for her opportunity, she had arrived.

Josephine telephoned Mike at Ford's at Boreham where he prepared cars for competitions and autosport events. She explained that Peter had rung her, that he wanted her for a modelling assignment, that she was to meet him at Witham. Could he be home in time to look after the children? Her appointment was for 6.30pm so he wouldn't have to be too late.

Some time shortly after 6 o'clock Josephine in her black and white fur-trimmed coat, left the house, left Mike, left John, Paula and Claire. The children would be in bed by the time she got back but she'd see them in the morning, she told them.

But by morning Mike had contacted the police. Josephine hadn't returned. Nor was there any sign of her on the Wednesday or the Thursday. On Friday, 1st November, three days after her disappearance, two Post-Office engineers found her fully-clothed body on the Essex-Hertfordshire border, 30 miles from Maldon, in lonely Bury Green Lane at Little Hadham, near Bishops Stortford. She lay face down in a shallow pond, her hands tightly bound in front of her. She had been manually strangled although there was a cord around her neck. There were no signs of sexual assualt. Police found her shoulder bag nearby. Her wrist watch had stopped at 8.10. There was some forensic evidence to suggest that she might have been alive when she was thrown out of a car.

Local people were horrified that so vivacious a woman, so respected a person, should end this way. She had been an asset to her community, a contributor. Many expressed their feelings publicly at such a loss.

The unsolved murder of Josephine Backshall remains one of this country's most puzzling cases. The police set up a mammoth investigation involving both Essex and Herts forces, led by Detective Chief Superintendent Ronald Harvey and Detective

Superintendent Jack Moulder, both of the Herts CID. There were some leads, admittedly frail; there were witnesses; there was a reconstruction; over 2,000 members of the public were interviewed; models, advertising agencies, photographers were visited and questioned; spread over many months, 100,000 man-hours of police time were expended. But no one was ever arrested. In such cases the police sometimes have an idea of the murderer's identity but are unable to make a charge for lack of evidence. In the case of Josephine Backshall, however, the extensive enquiries led nowhere. The mysterious man who had made phone calls to the house in Norfolk Close, who had even visited the house for a photo-session, was never found.

That Josephine Backshall drove to the Collingwood Road car park in Witham is not in dispute. It is quite certain that on the night of her disappearance she was the woman whose car bonnet was open in that car park as if she was experiencing some engine trouble. She refused the offer of help from a witness to whom she explained that someone would be coming along shortly to help her. Presumably she thought Peter would be able to resolve the difficulty. The police who found her car in the park thought she had been having trouble with a headlight.

There was some optimism when another witness, Raymond Robertson, came forward to say that he had seen a woman arguing with a young man wearing a checked sports jacket in the car park on the evening she had gone to her appointment. The man, Mr Robertson said, was about six feet tall. He also mentioned that the man's hair was short, quite contrary to the style of 1974. 'The woman looked as if she didn't want to get too close to him although he had his arm around her,' Robertson said. Was this Josephine? Was this Peter preparing to take her on a last car ride? Was he forcing her into his car? As Josephine's watch stopped at 8.10 pm, about an hour after this car park incident, had he bundled her in and driven with her straight to Little Hadham?

Or had she willingly entered the car, expecting to be taken to the modelling assignment? Were there stops on the way? An autopsy revealed that sometime after leaving home Josephine had eaten a meal consisting of white cabbage, beans, potato and mince. Shepherd's pie? A Chinese meal? But where had she eaten and when? Had she – and this seems most likely – eaten with the man who killed her? But a search of over a hundred restaurants, cafes, take-aways and pubs serving meals was abortive.

Joan Jones, landlady at the Fountain in Good Easter, shown photographs and holiday cinefilms of Josephine, was convinced that she was in the saloon bar on the night of 29th October and that she was accompanied by a tall man. They drank no more than a half-pint of bitter each. 'I remembered her at once,' she said. 'She was an attractive woman. She sat in the corner of the bar with the man and seemed totally at her ease.' This certainly does not tally with the description of the woman who only a short time before had been seen arguing in the car park.

The couple stayed at the Fountain for only a short time but Mrs Jones was of the view that the man contrived to keep his back to her. It was as if he was trying to avoid being seen. Was this hindsight on the part of the pub landlady? Was the man's behaviour so overtly suspicious? If he was so anxious not be seen, why in the first place did he go into the Fountain?

During the investigation no public mention was made of the Fountain visit. Perhaps the man believed to have been seen there with Josephine Backshall would feel confident enough to go back if he believed the police to be unaware of his having been there. But although the pub was kept under observation for long weeks there was never a hint of the man's presence.

This couple was seen to leave the pub in what some witnesses identified as a blue Ford. But further laborious checking of the registration numbers of hundreds of blue Fords produced nothing of value to this investigation.

Although the pub at Good Easter was on the route to Little Hadham where Josephine's body was found, there must be some doubt that she and her killer ever stopped there. Was there time for food, drink and a drive of 20 miles or so before 8.10 pm, if that was the time when Josephine was murdered? Nevertheless, the Fountain sighting seemed a positive enough lead for the police to pursue.

Police enquiries revealed the existence of a number of men who regularly scoured the advertisement columns of newspapers in the hope that they might offer the possibility of sexual adventures. Some of these advertisements are blatant. Their wording, sometimes coy, often challenging, leaves no room for doubt that sex is on offer. Other advertisements which at first seem wholly innocent contain a subtext of suggestion.

Was there anything in Josephine Backshall's advertisement

which might have encouraged some sexual predator to approach her? Did those words 'Anything considered' carry some hidden promise? Was someone disappointed to learn all too late that for Josephine Backshall this phrase indicated that she would consider tackling any kind of work appropriate to her experience and nothing more? Did this trusting woman naively encourage someone whose intentions were quite the opposite to hers?

In the course of their investigations, the police found other women in the district who had also been offered opportunities to model after inserting a wholly innocent advertisement in the newspaper. A man calling himself Peter had offered the prospect of modelling work to three women who had advertised in local newspapers. They had all rejected him.

Another woman had been telephoned twice in July 1974 by a man who claimed that he was about to open a shop selling toilet requisites. They arranged to meet in a car park at Bishops Stortford but he failed to arrive. This witness was unsure of the caller's name; she thought that it might have been Johnson, Thompson or Jennings.

In September, two women living in villages near Colchester were similarly approached. They too had advertised for work and the man told them that he intended opening a toiletries shop in Colchester. Meetings were arranged at local railway stations but the caller failed to turn up.

In the Backshall house police found some samples of perfumes from France. On his visit to the house had Peter left these with Josephine as some kind of proof of his claims to be a cosmetics salesman? Had he suggested that they were a batch to be used in a sales drive? But though the perfumes might have been at first considered a useful lead nothing came of it.

And the killer? Was his behaviour not unusual? Why did he fail to turn up to meet Josephine on two occasions? Did he not think that this might deter his victim from ever meeting him? Or was his conscience on those evenings stronger than his appetites? On the other hand, was this all part of his game? Was stalking Josephine Backshall part of the thrill, watching her as she arrived at the car park? Was there an extra frisson to be had from visiting her at her home? This was, as the police said, a man with nerves of steel, confident of his power, a very dangerous man.

Even the name he had used was uncertain. Was he Johnson, Thompson or Jennings? Was he Peter or David? In reality he might have been none of these. But people bearing combinations of these names had to be considered. In those pre-computer days, slow and painstaking searches through old filing systems were required. And produced nothing.

Josephine Backshall, that attractive, cheerful woman who was described by a neighbour as 'just a normal, everyday housewife, interested in her home and family', was only seeking a little pin-money. It would have been used for the girls' dresses, for her son's cycle, perhaps for some small luxuries for her husband and herself. But the man who spotted her advertisement had his needs too and they were paramount.

Was he the man who called several other women, the man who offered modelling assignments, the man who intended to open up a toiletries business in Colchester? It does seem likely. And was Josephine Backshall, whose trusting nature led to her death, his sole victim? It is difficult to think so.

It is not so long ago really. He may still be alive, this man who called himself Peter, in his early thirties in 1974; a tall man, heavily built; knowledgeable about perfumes and women's toiletries; a highly competent photographer. Is he still about?

A FIRE AT THE
SHIRE HALL

THE football club's great day has probably been long forgotten but the dreadful and mysterious incident of that same evening in 1938 has been resurrected from time to time. For how was it that a happy, young, cake-shop manageress unaccountably burst into flames? How was it that she was so swiftly engulfed in fire in front of several astonished witnesses? Spontaneous human combustion? Can it have been so?

But to 27th August, 1938. For Chelmsford City Football Club, this was a red letter day, a day when the club was taking a significant step forward in its search for recognition. For the first time they had played against the more prestigious Bristol Rovers Reserves and to acknowledge such a triumph the Supporters' Club arranged a Saturday night celebration dance in the Shire Hall. It went off very well. There was no drunkenness though admittedly there was some slight unpleasantness, some of the young bulls locking horns, but nothing to spoil the evening for the majority of those attending. And when the dance came to its end at midnight – there were very few chances of dances going on into the early hours of Sunday in 1938 – people went off to collect their coats from the downstairs cloakrooms and make for home. But there was something of a crush and Phyllis Newcombe and her fiance, Henry McAusland, hung back in the ballroom until it had partially cleared.

Only when it had did they make their way to the door to the landing, Henry leading the way to the top of the staircase, Phyllis a few steps behind him. And then he heard the scream, turned and saw that the front of Phyllis's dress was alight. He saw her run back as if towards the ballroom they had just left, before collapsing. Others too had heard the cry. Several footballers and one of the club directors, Hector Jewell, ran to the fallen girl. The

The Shire Hall, Chelmsford, where in 1938 a young woman inexplicably became engulfed in flames.

flames were roaring fiercely now and only with some difficulty were the men able to quench it, Henry trying to beat out the flames with his bare hands and others throwing their jackets and overcoats across the body of the prostrate girl.

Eventually, suffering from extensive burns, Phyllis was taken to the manager's office to await the arrival of the ambulance to take her to Chelmsford Hospital where for several days, she lingered on. Indeed at one stage she seemed on the point of recovery, but on 15th September she relapsed and died. Phyllis Newcombe was 22 years of age.

The *Essex Chronicle* of 2nd September gave an account of the accident, attributing the cause of the fire to 'the throwing down of a lighted match or cigarette end which burst into flames.' This idea seems to have been generally accepted. Although there had been no drunkenness, drink was available and doubtless someone had taken enough to be careless. Presumably Phyllis's long, billowing crinoline style dress of white tulle with its satin under-skirt had simply flared up.

At the inquest, held in the Shire Hall where the incident had occurred, the Coroner pursued the matter of smoking with Henry McAusland, asking if anyone nearby might have been accidentally responsible.

-When you heard her scream was there anybody near her?
-No, sir.
-Was she smoking?
-No, neither of us was.
-Were there any cigarette ends on the floor?
-I hardly had a chance to look around.

A constable who had been called to the scene said that there were some cigarette ends on the floor in the area where the incident occurred but that was quite usual.

The Coroner hoped, however, that Phyllis when in hospital might have given McAusland some clue to the cause.

-Did she say anything at all?
-Not at the time of the accident. After the first week in hospital she was making quite good progress but she did not suggest any cause of the accident. I said I would like to know the careless devil who threw that cigarette end away and she said, 'What does it matter as long as I get better?'

Perhaps, the Coroner mused, the sides of Phyllis's crinoline-style dress stuck out. Perhaps a cigarette end might have accidentally touched it, causing it to flare up suddenly, 'with the tragic results that we have heard.'

He pondered the possibility of deliberately silly behaviour. 'I was just thinking of some persons with a perverted sense of humour who might have done something as a kind of lark. There are quite a number of people about who have a perverted sense of humour. Just imagine someone dropping a lighted match on that rubber floor. It would certainly go on burning.' But he seemed to give up on that idea. 'If nothing was found it is no use theorising about it. It is a very extraordinary thing. I cannot conceive a lighted cigarette end being the cause unless it was dropped by someone onto her dress.'

Henry McAusland told the court that the dress had been cleaned twice, once about six weeks before the dance. Perhaps, he suggested, traces of benzine in the material had rendered it dangerously inflammable. But many dresses at many dances were fresh from the cleaners: were they all so vulnerable to fire? There had been no other instances reported and this suggestion was not seriously pursued by the court. (Michael Harrison, author of *Fire from Heaven*, refers to another case where a girl attempted to clean a dress by immersing it in a bath of benzine. As she rinsed the dress there was a sudden explosion which hurled her backwards, singeing her eyebrows and hair. But there was no fire and the dress was not even scorched.)

So could a match or cigarette thrown from the balcony which overlooked the landing have set fire to it, the Coroner mused before going out to inspect the landing. On his return he was no wiser. 'I am afraid I can make nothing of it at all,' he said. 'Nothing could have come from the balcony without anyone noticing it and it is not directly over the landing but over the stairs.' It was all very bewildering.

George Newcombe, the father of Phyllis, told the court that he had experimented at home with material from Phyllis's dress. He produced a piece of the white material. It would not ignite, he told the court, even when it was soaked in petrol. When in court he touched the dress with a lit cigarette, it burned a hole in the material but did not burst into flame. The Coroner then produced a cigarette lighter and applied it to the dress material. It caught fire at once. But at the dance there had been no possibility of a cigarette lighter being used on Phyllis Newcombe's dress.

The cause of death according to the Home Office pathologist, Francis Camps, was pneumonia, secondary to toxaemia, secondary to extensive burns on the upper part of the body. A verdict of Accidental Death was returned. It was recorded by the Coroner that the clothing had caught fire for some unknown reason. 'I must say,' he added, 'that in all my experience I have not met with anything so very mysterious as this.'

But one thing was certain as far as the Coroner was concerned. '*Obviously this is not spontaneous combustion*,' he said. But why not? Because in the opinion of the Coroner – and not just that Coroner's opinion in 1938 but that of very many Coroners, medical men and fire officers today – there was no such thing.

Spontaneous human combustion is so often rejected as a possible cause of unexplained fires. It is an absurdity, it is said, a figment of the imagination, a ludicrous fancy propagated by novelists. Dickens, of course, had one of his characters, Krook in *Bleak House*, burst into flame and burn to a cinder. But it was not all fiction, the novelist declared. He had also collected what he claimed were 30 genuine cases of SHC.

Down the years there have been many cases from all over the

world about which claims of SHC have been made. And the claims are simply that without warning, people have burst into flame.

Like many of the cases experienced in Britain, Phyllis Newcombe's body was not completely consumed by the fire. There have been several instances where others have been able to quench the flames in time. Some of those saved, however, later died in hospital. What is remarkable in such cases is that those who have been able to speak after their experience have never been able to say what really happened to them at the time. This has been a curiously consistent factor. Not only have bystanders been taken by surprise but the victims themselves have been equally bewildered. This is what renders such occurrences the more remarkable. They have puzzled not only Coroners as in the Shire Hall in Chelmsford but also doctors, policemen and fire officers. Despite their dismay and lack of answers, however, there has always been a powerful rejection of such a seemingly outrageous suggestion.

All sorts of theories have been advanced to explain the cause of this baffling phenomenon. Victims have taken too much drink, has been one answer to the mystery. They have stumbled and fallen head first into the fireplace. But even if this is the answer to some cases of SHC, it was not so in the case of Phyllis Newcombe. She had not taken an excess of alcohol. There was certainly no externally obvious source of fire. Or was she carrying a box of matches in her pocket which suddenly took fire? Apparently not, but even if she were would this have accounted for so sudden a combustion?

Scientists who have worked on the subject have focused on three possibilities. Is there some release of nuclear energy in the body, something likened to a small nuclear explosion, which produces a violent heat which consumes the body, the fire originating on the inside?

Or are there in certain bodies excessively high amounts of gas within the gut and does this in some way trigger combustion within the digestive system? Does diet occasionally produce from our cocktail of foods and drinks a combustible gas? Does some kind of chemical reaction cause a mini-fireball to rage with unexpected suddenness in the abdomen of SHC victims?

Perhaps it is that some people possess an abnormal amount of electricity within them. There are, after all, instances of people who can quite unintentionally affect the operation of televisions and computers. Is there some untapped electrical energy which erupts? Perhaps this can in the course of a normally active life be worked off but perhaps in the case of the old or sedentary such stored-up energy cannot be worked off and eventually can only be released in some violent manner.

Did Phyllis Newcombe suffer some kind of internal explosion of the kind described above? Perhaps. Though, as she had been dancing the night away, she would presumably have worked off the effects of an earlier meal and any excess electrical energy.

The whole issue of spontaneous human combustion is a problem. A Coroner, enquiring into the death of a Folkestone man in 1987, did not rule out the possibility. Yet there are scores of other cases which defy any rational explanation. Several cases from all parts of the world, raised now to the status of classics of their kind, have baffled the experts. In 1744 an Ipswich woman burst into flames in front of her daughter; in 1904, a woman in Falkirk was burned beyond recognition, sitting in a chair in her own house; in 1930, a New York woman was burned to death fully clothed in her own house though her clothing was untouched by fire; in 1938 a girl dancing in a Soho nightclub burst into flames, the flames coming from her back, shoulders and chest. And so on. How can these be explained? How can the case of the Kirby sisters of Sowerby Bridge be understood? In 1899 the two little girls were a mile apart, in different houses, when at 11 o'clock in the morning they simultaneously burst into flames and were both consumed by fire. The Coroner was bemused. Naturally so. And so are we today by this remarkable occurrence. Was this spontaneous human combustion? How else can it be explained?

And the Phyllis Newcombe case is still a cause of mystery. How could a young woman have so suddenly been attacked by fire in this inexplicable manner? If this Chelmsford incident was not a case of spontaneous human combustion, what was it?

A Ghost of a Christmas Past

Christmas Day.
Christmas tree.
And under the tree the woman's body.
And it is Minka who finds her sprawled there. It is 10-year-old Minka Kokas who finds her mother, a suicide, dead from a lethal cocktail of heroin, alcohol, pills.
But this Christmas Day tragedy does not end here for there, on the floor, is what Minka thinks at first is a Christmas card.
But it is not a Christmas card even though it is addressed to Minka. It is her mother's goodbye note.
And it reads: 'I never wanted you anyway and look what you have done to me. You are the worst thing I ever did. I hope you are satisfied.'
Minka's father had died of cancer the previous year.
Christmas card; Christmas tree; Christmas Day 1979.

ORPHANED now, young Minka was fortunate to be fostered at Leigh-on-Sea by a former midwife who gave the child abundant love and security. Nevertheless, all through the succeeding years of childhood, adolescence and young woman-hood, Minka was somehow aware of her mother's presence. She grew up with a feeling of unease, with the sense of someone else in the house with her. There seemed in some strange way to be constant hints, regular suggestions, that her mother, Yvonne, was never far away. Always, it seemed, there were the faintest reminders for Minka of her unhappy past, small, unaccountable features which disturbed her life. For example, Minka had brought a bedroom lamp with her from her childhood home. Why had it intermittently over the years made curious noises in the night? By itself, perhaps of little consequence. But there were so many inconsequential elements in Minka's life.

When her foster mother died, the house at Leigh-on-Sea where she had experienced so much love and kindness was left to Minka, now a model and beautician. And it was from that time that the awareness of her mother's presence became gradually even more overpowering. Sometimes there were odd smells, what Minka was to describe as her mother's cheap perfume, her mother's booze, her mother's chihuahuas which as a child she had so disliked. And more and more she was aware of some uncanny presence in her home. Unsurprisingly, Minka was terrified. The mother who had so damaged her childhood had, she believed, come to persecute her.

And then there was the voice. Minka was to say that she thought she could hear her mother's voice although she could not make out precisely what words were being spoken. But she was sure that her mother was trying to contact her. 'I just knew she was trying to reach me,' she said. What was it that she was trying to say? Was she trying to tell her daughter yet again how much she had hated her, how much she held her responsible for her death?

Even Minka's boyfriend, Eddie, appears to have been affected by Yvonne. One night in 1997 he suddenly sat bolt upright in bed and announced that they should go to put flowers on Yvonne's grave. It was an indescribably odd suggestion that, in the middle of the night, seemed to come out of nowhere. Eddie and Minka had not earlier in the evening been discussing Yvonne and they seem never to have given the matter of putting flowers on the grave any previous consideration.

On another occasion when Eddie was in bed on his own, the music box which he had bought for Minka's 21st birthday began playing of its own accord. Not unnaturally he was alarmed and was on the point of smashing it when, just as suddenly as the music had begun, it stopped.

Then there was the time when Minka was going on holiday to Scotland and as she was leaving her house, she announced in a light-hearted fashion, 'Look after the house for me.' It was the kind of joky, inconsequential remark that anyone leaving for holiday in high spirits might make.

No sooner had Minka left than her two cats disappeared, much to the anguish of a friend who had been asked to look in on the house during Minka's absence. Yet on the day of her return from holiday, the cats also came back. Coincidence? Not according to

Minka whose view was that her throw-away remark to the empty house had been an invitation for her mother's spirit to take possession. And hadn't Yvonne detested cats? Was this not perhaps the reason for their staying away from the house until Minka came back?

And her good friend, looking in on the house on the last day of Minka's holiday just to ensure that all was well, and going about her neighbourly duties, was suddenly terrified. The lights in the house started turning themselves on and off. Unnerved, she ran out of the house.

Even so, until the mid-1990s, the hauntings were not on a regular basis. But then they reached a new, increased level. Where once they had been spasmodic they now intensified and over the succeeding months Minka became increasingly desperate, terrified of the presence in the house which she did not doubt was her mother. She could not control what was happening in her own home, fearing her mother's spirit and hating it too. She believed that she was going mad. Or being driven mad.

The bizarre occurrences went on and on. For example, when Minka was putting up the Christmas tree in December 1998, the volume of the stereo which was playing suddenly went down. Had she accidentally knocked the remote control, Eddie asked her. Seemed feasible, he thought. Or at least that is what he told her he thought. But Minka knew that she had been nowhere near the control, which was on the sideboard. And then one night in early 1999, when she was in the house alone, an electric light bulb exploded. Oh yes, the terrified Minka Kokas knew what was behind all of these curious happenings. How long would her torment last? Was she to be plagued in this way for ever and ever?

And then, quite remarkably, along came a change in Minka's fortunes. The BBC2 television series *Modern Times* was investigating the supernatural and hearing of Minka's story went to interview her. It was a significant occasion in the course of which the television team persuaded Minka that she ought to attempt to get to the bottom of this seemingly mischievous and malignant series of happenings. Perhaps if she sought the cause some remedy might be possible. She made arrangements to see a leading psychic in London.

The meeting with the psychic astonished Minka. Could she remember that her mother was known to her friends not as Yvonne but as Von, she was asked? Yes, of course she could. But she had never thought of that version of her mother's name for many years. How amazing it was to be told about something so remotely tucked away in her memory.

The whole occasion was remarkable, Minka was to recall later. She felt sick; every hair on her body seemed to stand on end as the psychic explained to her that all of these 20 years Yvonne, whose memory and whose presence she had come to fear and loathe, had been trying to contact her. Not that Yvonne was seeking forgiveness but she desperately wanted her daughter to understand that on that Christmas morning when she had penned the cruel letter to her only child, on that day of all days when she had taken her own life, she had not been in total command of herself. Minka had to understand that. She had not intended to be so cruel. And as for her attempts to get into contact, to explain matters to her daughter, these were never intended to frighten.

It was at this point that Minka finally came to understand the cause of this paranormal activity. And it was then that she felt what she described as a great 'whoosh' of energy after which she felt cleansed. 'It was,' she said, 'as if I had been exorcised.' Her mother had not intended to terrify: those 20 years she had been trying to explain. Perhaps, Minka has since thought, her mother actually protected her when some years earlier she had been in a horrifying car crash. The police had actually expected to find Minka decapitated but she says that somehow, at the last moment, a strange impulse told her to curl up and this saved her from serious injury. Was that Yvonne offering some kind of warning? 'If it was my mother,' she says, 'it was the one good thing her spirit did for me.'

All of the eerie happenings have now stopped. Life is normal after so many years of anxiety. There are no more smells or voices. The various eccentric electrical tricks are no longer experienced. Minka Kokas has visited her mother's grave with flowers. And Yvonne, her message delivered, is now at peace.

BIBLIOGRAPHY

Andrew Collins, *The Aveley Abduction; Flying Saucer Review*
Vols 23, 24: 1978
Trevor Dearing, *It's True*, Mohr Books 1996
John C. Dening, *The Restless Spirits of Langenhoe*, Self published
2000
Wesley H. Downes, *Essex Collection of Ghosts and Hauntings*,
Wesley 1993
Adrian Gray, *Tales of Old Essex*, Countryside Books 1987
Melvin Harris, *The True Face of Jack the Ripper*, Michael
O'Mara Books 1994
Michael Harrison, *Fire from Heaven*, Pan 1976
John E. Heymer, *The Entrancing Flame*, Little, Brown 1996
Stephen Knight, *Jack the Ripper: The Final Solution*, Harrap 1976
W. E. Liddell and Michael Howard, *The Pickingill Papers*, Capall
Bann 1994
Eric Maple, *The Dark World of Witches*, Robert Hale 1962
Brian McConnell, *The Possessed*, Brockhampton Press 1995
Harry Price, *Poltergeist over England*, Country Life 1945
Jenny Randles, *Alien Contact*, Collins and Brown 1997
Jenny Randles, *Time Storms*, Piatkus 2001
Jenny Randles and Peter Hough, *Spontaneous Human
Combustion*, Robert Hale 1992
William J. T. Smith, *The Boreham Witch – Fact or Fiction?*, Self
published 1995
Philip Sugden, *The Complete History of Jack the Ripper*, Carroll
and Graff 1995
Paul Tabori and Peter Underwood, *The Ghosts of Borley*, David
and Charles 1973
David Thurlow, *The Essex Triangle*, Robert Hale 1990
G. H. Totterdell, *Country Copper*, Harrap 1956
Robert Wood, *The Widow of Borley*, Duckworth 1992

The author has also consulted a wide variety of newspapers and
magazines, both local and national, including *True Detective* magazine.